For You

Andreas Seidl

Handover of Power

Global Version

Volume 5: Digital

Imprint

Bibliographic information of the German National Library: The German National Library lists this publication in the German National Bibliography; detailed bibliographic data are available on the Internet at http://dnb.dnb.de.

© 2022 Dipl. Pol. Theodor Andreas Seidl

Cover: Christiane Ebrecht
Translation: DeepL, Cologne
Production and publishing: BoD – Books on Demand, Norderstedt

ISBN: 978-3-7568-1335-3

Acknowledgements

My thanks go to my family and friends who have made me who I am today. Special thanks to all those who supported me in writing this book. I would like to thank all my classmates, teachers, fellow students, lecturers, demonstrators, activists, colleagues, companies and countries with whom I have had the privilege of sharing the experiences from which all the ideas in this book have emerged. I would like to thank the staff of Books on Demand for their kind helpfulness. I thank the citizens of Seligenstadt for the harmony and solidarity in which I was able to write.

Foreword

This policy concept contains a variety of proposals for possible political reforms. It can be peacefully and democratically adapted to any current political system of any state in the world, but also to political systems in families, clubs, associations or companies. Wherever humans make or submit to rules that manage living together, the following proposals can be helpful. Readers who find the proposals so helpful that they would like to implement them together with like-minded people can contact the author. The contact form on the last page can be used for this purpose.

Faults and defects

I ask for your understanding that this volume was not professionally proofread. I could only afford professional proofreading for the summary. Spelling errors and unfortunate phrasing may therefore occur. As soon as this volume has sold enough to pay for a professional proofreading, it will be done. After that, a new edition will be published.

English version

Please understand that this volume has been translated automatically. I could only afford a professional translation for the summary. Poor wording and spelling errors may therefore occur. In case of doubt, the German version shall prevail. As soon as this volume has sold enough to pay for a professional translation, it will be done. After that, a new edition will be published. It was more important to me that no one in the world should have an information advantage than individual translation errors in the complete work.

References

If something has been quoted directly, it is set in italics. If the headings contain footnotes, the sources for direct and indirect quotations apply in the chapter for which the heading stands. Otherwise, quotations or source references are directly at the word or at the end of the sentence or paragraph. This book contains parts of text based on the Federal Constitution of the Swiss Confederation of 18 April 1999 (as of 12 February 2017), abbreviated to BV[1] and the Constitution of the Canton of Bern of 6 June 1993 (as of 11 March 2015), abbreviated to KV[2] .

If the constitutional paragraph, or individual paragraphs thereof, are based in whole or in part on extracts from the BV or KV, this is indicated in a footnote. The references to the corresponding footnotes for constitutional paragraphs are usually found after the heading of the affected chapter and sometimes in the body of the text. Articles used in the Swiss constitutions are listed in the footnote with a number after the title of the constitutional paragraph. Example: §123 Sample title: BV Art.123, KV Art.123.

All internet sources are fully cited in the footnotes. They were last accessed on 30.09.2021. All literature sources are also listed in full in the footnotes.

All references to tasks undertaken by other ministries and described in more detail there are given in footnotes. Example: Model Ministry - 1.2.3 Model Chapter.

All footnotes are to be viewed in comparison to the respective source, so-called indirect quotations. Direct quotations are set in italics, but hardly ever occur. The source reference is intended to enable further investigation and to take copyright

---

1 This is not an official publication. Only the publication by the Swiss Federal Chancellery is authoritative. https://www.fedlex.admin.ch/eli/cc/1999/404/de On 14.12.2021

2 This is not an official publication. The Bernese Official Collection of Laws is authoritative. https://www.belex.sites.be.ch/frontend/versions/2420?locale=de#ART71 On 16.12.2021

into account.

Table of contents

1 Goals of the Ministry of Digital Affairs

The aim of the Ministry of Digital Affairs is to enable a virtual civil society that is involved in opinion-forming and legislation. The state with its ministries and governments thus receives a virtual image of the inland, consisting of personal, technical and geographical data. With this image, the state is able to carry out a policy simulation for the future effects of today's deciders. Big data is dangerous if the data is not subject to democratic control.

Big Data means that personal data is stored en masse and correlated with each other. But it is a great way to make policy. So far, Big Data is mainly known for enterprise policy decisions to use customer data to create market analyses in order to sell more. The intranet is a state citizen platform that uses citizen data for state policy decisions in order to create analyses of the people in order to govern in the interest of the common good.

Ensuring the security and protection of data and digital content constantly at the highest possible level is a significant goal of the Ministry of Digital Affairs. Equally important, however, is taking advantage of the fact that digital data can be copied and shared as often as desired. To ease this tension, the Ministry of Digital Affairs uses the mentality of open source systems, also called "open source". This community practice is copied and supported by the Ministry of Digital Affairs. In the open source community, volunteers create operating systems, programmes and updates free of charge for all users. Creators and users help each other find and fix faults in the systems.

The aim is to be able to offer more voting procedures more frequently and more cheaply, but at the same time to prevent multiple voting. Similarly, state news should no longer have to be sent in paper form by post to a fixed address. Companies and persons should also be allowed to use the devices and the intranet, because the infrastructure exists anyway and use for economic purposes is in the interest of the national economy and helps to link the economic forms.

The medium-term goal is to expand the domestic citizens' intranet to include the continental intranet.

The long-term goal is to set up a global intranet in the united states of the world while maintaining data security. How quickly this happens will be decided by the citizens, because this is about trust and not just about policy integration. Separation is easy because the data and systems can be encrypted or decrypted.

2 Departments

The departments are divided into sub-departments and enumerations are usually considered as their individual units. Many tasks of some departments are completely taken over by other ministries as a service.

2.1 Central Department

Part of the Central Department is the Reception Office with the Courier and Mail Room, which directs all concerns, broadcasts and visitors to the appropriate place in the ministry.

2.1.1 Staff

The Human Resources Department is responsible for staff development and planning. For this purpose, it takes care of the recruitment of junior staff, intern and trainee programmes as well as the selection procedures for employees and special selection procedures for applicants with disabilities. For politicians and employees, the department prepares a job plan. In all its tasks, it works in voting with the personnel board.[1]

All other personnel matters are transferred to the relevant ministries. The Ministry of Education is responsible for the training and further education of employees for the state service.[2] The Ministry of Labour takes over the service law.[3] This includes labour and collective bargaining law for employees in the state service, remuneration, personnel

---

1 Ministry of State Organisation - 2.1.1.1 Personnel board
2 Ministry of Education - 2.1.1.1 Education and training for the state service
3 Ministry of Labour - 4 State enterprises, 13 Labour Directory

administration of all careers and employees, flexitime, holiday and sick leave, working time with or without flexitime in part-time or full-time at the place of work or in home work. The Ministry of Infrastructure provides housing assistance for all state employees.[4] The Ministry of Finance's Pay Office takes care of employees' salary, expenses, travel and relocation costs.[5] The Ministry of Education provides childcare for all employees in the state service.[6]

The Ministry of Health is responsible for the occupational health service.[7] It ensures occupational health management, deals with the treatment, education and prevention of occupational accidents, controls and provides occupational health and safety through the health auditors[8] of the Company Auditing Agency[9] .

2.1.2 Organisation

The ministries of media, security, justice, finance, labour, state organisation provide audit services for quality management in the ministry, evaluation of work performance, revenues and expenditures, as well as corruption prevention, sabotage protection and, if necessary, disciplinary matters.[10]

The Ministry of Labour regulates procurement law and ensures corruption-free state orders and procurement.[11] The Ministry of Finance organises the annual budget vote and ensures proper accounting in each ministry.[12] It regulates budget procedures, budget law, staff budgets, departmental budgets, costs and cash management, and assists ministries in budget planning for the budget vote. The language service for translating talks or texts is provided by the Ministry of

---

4 Ministry of Infrastructure - 2.1.1.1 Housing assistance for state service employees
5 Ministry of Finance - 2.1.1.1 Staff remuneration
6 Ministry of Education - 2.1.1.2 Childcare for state service employees
7 Ministry of Health - 2.1.1.1 Occupational Health Service
8 Ministry of Labour - 20.7.2 Health auditor
9 Ministry of Labor - 20 Company Auditing Agency
10 Ministries of Media, Security, Justice, Finance, State Organisation - 2.1.2.1 Audit services
11 Ministry of Labour - 6 Procurement Office
12 Ministry of Finance - 8 state revenues, 9 state expenditure

Education.[13]

2.1.2.1 Digital service[14]

The digital service handles all the tasks that other ministries have to do in their digital administration. Information technicians and system administrators work in the digital service. They support all ministries with Information Technology and enable the ministers to manage their ministry digitally.

2.1.2.1.1 Supporting the supply of Information Technology

Technicians ensure the procurement, provision, maintenance and service of technical devices and software. Applicable data protection in information and communication technology is taken into account in the construction and programming of hardware and software. Information technology and digitalisation officers are responsible for rectifying faults or breaches of data protection. Programmes and algorithms support and coordinate appointment calendars of all state service employees and automatically handle the documentation service. The documentary is stored in the digital state archive and can be used by all ministries for further processing. Citizens can constantly consult this documentary through the historical service in the ministries' library.

2.1.2.1.2 Election advertising

For the purposes of election advertising, the digital service does commissioned work for parties. Anyone who draws up an election manifesto for the election of persons[15] can commission election advertising. All applicants who stand for pre-election receive the same quota of working hours from the digital service. It is up to each candidate to decide how much of this he or she wants to use. In the field service, the

---

13 Ministry of Education - 2.1.3 Language Service
14 §46.5 State, §71.2.4 Review of effectiveness: BV Art.170
15 Ministry of State Organisation - 9.9.4.4 Programme election campaign

web designers work with the principals to develop content for election advertising, such as websites, PC games, browser games or apps. In the indoor service, this content is then programmed and made available on party websites and intranet pages.

2.2 Management Department

The Management Department is the minister's department. With his office team, he provides policy planning and analysis for his ministry and coordinates the relationship between the nation and the municipality through exchanges with his deputies in the municipalities. He initiates cooperation with other ministries or citizens in committees and is supported by the Ministry of State Organisation.
The Ministry of Media Affairs, through its media service, provides press and public relations for the ministry, moderates civil dialogue, trains or provides a spokesperson for the minister, writes speeches and texts on request, and ensures the implementation of conferences and events.[16]

2.2.1 Digital management

Ministers can administer departmental management digitally via a Content Management System (CMS). Business statistics are automatically compiled from all directories and profiles. Staff surveys are conducted and evaluated. Video telephony is possible for enquiries. The current state of research, including statistics, concerning the ministry's remit can be retrieved. The current state of research for the other ministries is collected by the Ministry of Education[17] through its researchers and forwarded to the Ministry of Digital Affairs. Proposals from staff and citizens are forwarded to responsible offices via the intranet and answered. The Company Auditing Agency's audits are used for regular data collection. The data are forwarded to the Ministry of Digital Affairs together with evaluations.

---

16 Ministry of Media Affairs - 2.2.1.1 Media Service
17 Ministry of Education - 11.7.2 State research institutes

Document management and forms are available via a link to the ministries' library.

2.3 Digital Department

The Digital Department, in cooperation with all ministries and the Statistical Office, ensures the bundling and distribution of all data for statistical measurement. It operates the State Archives, the Access Directory, the Institute for Information Security and the interfaces between the Intranet and the Internet. It supervises the Statistical Office.
In voting with the Digital Minister, the Digital Department formulates the legal templates for digital data, administration, data protection, crime and business on the internet and intranet.

2.4 Intranet Department

The Intranet Department ensures the operation of the Intranet in cooperation with the Ministry of Infrastructure. It commissions the People's Innovation Company[18] Intranet to programme applications, programmes, operating systems and computer games on behalf of the Minister of Digital Affairs, other ministries or their agencies. In cooperation with the respective ministries, it ensures the operation of the directories. In cooperation with the Ministry of Innovation, it operates the People's Innovation Company Intranet and ensures its adequate funding and the secured production of People's Computers. In voting with the Minister of Digital Affairs, it formulates templates for regularisation of the People's Computer, programmes and computer games. In cooperation with the Ministry of Security, it locates and secures lost or tampered People's Computers and voting computers. The Intranet Department runs the Intranet Cafés in the town halls.

---

18 Ministry of Innovation - 10 People's Innovation Company

3 Tasks of the Ministry of Digital Affairs[19]

The Ministry of Digital Affairs is responsible for promoting the digitalisation of the state and its citizens. To digitise the state, it operates the digital service, which supports all ministries with telecommunications technology and its handling. To connect the ministries with each other and with the citizens, the Ministry of Digital Affairs operates the intranet, intranet cafés in the town halls, directories and the People's Innovation Company Intranet for the production of hardware and software.

The task of the Ministry of Digital Affairs is the legal regularisation of digital matters, such as data, administration, statistics, data protection, crime or economy on the intranet and internet. For the fulfilment of the resulting tasks, the Ministry of Digital Affairs operates the State Archives, the Statistical Office, servers, the Access Directory, the Institute for Information Security and transfer facilities for data between the Intranet and the Internet.

For the operation of the intranet, the Ministry of Digital Affairs regulates the requirements and the process for admission to the intranet. It operates the People's Navigator with the help of the People's Innovation Company Intranet, with which users can operate the intranet. The People's Navigator fulfils the task of structuring the search, management and display on the playing field with its page structure in such a way that information and simulations are visible to the user. Avatars enable citizens to live out their lives digitally and to simulate several possibilities. For the directories, the People's Navigator fulfils the task of arranging them in a comprehensible structure for users.

The Ministry of Digital Affairs uses the intranet cafés to support citizens with telecommunications technology. The supply includes the sale, rental and repair of People's Innovation Company Intranet products. For elections and voting, the Ministry of Digital Affairs is responsible for operating the voting booths and voting computers in the intranet cafés.

With the operation of the directories, ministries and citizens are networked with and among each other. Through a unified

---

19§207.1 Telecommunications: BV Art. 92

structure of profiles and groups, posts, comments, responses and ratings, citizens can keep track of and organise their social, economic and political contacts.

The People's Innovation Company Intranet fulfils the task of producing devices, operating systems, programmes and computer games and distributing them via the Intranet cafés. It keeps the hardware and software constantly up to date and secures them from unauthorised access. The People's Computer is used to enable citizens from all over the country to participate in governance and store their data. With its programmes, the People's Innovation Company Intranet provides tools for handling the intranet and its directories. The People's Innovation Company Intranet computer games fulfil the task of the political management of the state by the citizens, the digitalisation of state services and the simulation of the future effects of personal, social, economic and political decisions.

4 Digital law[20]

Digital law consists of telecommunications, media and postal law. It applies in the real world as well as in radio transmissions, on the internet and on the intranet. The legal framework for digital services and the media industry is defined by the constitution as follows.

All Information Technology must guarantee freedom of expression and information. Every person must be able to form, express and disseminate his or her opinion freely and without hindrance. To this end, it is necessary to be able to receive and communicate information from freely available sources. Opinions and information must not be banned or censored in advance. Censorship is only permissible, if at all, if it means that a criminal offence can no longer be carried out or if owners of data arrange for it to be deleted. Especially when it comes to democratic expressions and voting on the intranet, the free formation of will and undistorted casting of votes must be guaranteed.

All nationals have the right to access all data collected

20§13 Freedom of expression and information: BV Art.16, KV Art.17, §14,1,2,3 Data protection: KV Art.18, §35,2 Political rights: BV Art.34

about them. The time delay is only permissible if there are investigative tactical reasons from an ongoing investigation or criminal proceedings. As soon as the proceedings have been concluded or discontinued, the report must be made at the latest. Any access to data by the user of a People's Computer shall be reported to him by an entry in his Access Directory. Authorities are allowed to require the entry of data needed to fulfil a state service. To do this, authorities must be authorised by a law and provide the owners of the data with the relevant law for viewing. This task is automatically taken over by the Access Directory.

4.1 Data ownership

Originators of data are considered to be its owners. When someone enters data, that data is their property. The person requesting the data entry must agree on a written treaty with the person who wants to enter the data before the data is entered. The treaty must stipulate what may be done with the data. If the person requesting data input uses the data, they must prove to the owner and the Company Auditing Agency's technical auditors that data protection is guaranteed. Data owners must be able to be informed at any time and without delay of what data they have already left with a user. If their data is not presented correctly, owners should request an immediate correction. Owners have the right to have their data deleted immediately, except for investigative reasons.

5 Digital administration

The entire administration of the state is digitised. The digital service is responsible for the digitisation of the administration and the People's Innovation Company Intranet provides the necessary information technology. In order to keep the technology up to date, digitisation programmes are carried out on an ongoing basis, provided that the people approve the costs in the budget vote.

The identity management of workers and citizens is carried out via the intranet in the Persons Directory and Labour

Directory, as well as via their passports and identity cards. In order to maintain integrity, all actions between citizens and the state must be carried out via the intranet and not via the internet.

To prevent corruption, payments by the state are processed through the People's Bank[21] , which must account for them to the people. Through the tax game and the budget vote, the state budget can be directly influenced by the citizen.[22] Orders and payments for government purchases must be made through the Procurement Office or the Administrative Office for Personnel and Inventory.[23]

For better making of law, the Ministry of Digital Affairs provides the necessary intranet applications, computer programmes and directories to make government decisions in uniform procedures with or without citizen participation. This also includes So-called standards screening. For this, anyone taking an initiative for a norm must have the template simulated by the Algoracle in order to test long-term consequences. Citizens can investigate and influence legislation via the veto quorum and norms via the Law Directory and the repeal quorum.[24]

5.1 State Archives

The State Archives is an internal alliance on the intranet so that all employees of every ministry can access it. Every data retrieval by a staff member in the same ministry or from other ministries is stored in the Access Directory of the State Archives.

For federal information management, all municipalities are in an alliance with each other and with the capital city. In this alliance, all data is stored in the State Archives The digital service ensures that the data is stored on central servers and on hard drives of the computers in the offices, depending on where the data can be better secured and protected.

---

21 Ministry of Finance - 11 People's Bank
22 Ministry of Finance - 11 People's Bank, 9.5 Budget vote, 9.6 Tax game
23 Ministry of Labour - 5 Administrative Office, 6 Procurement Office
24 Ministry of Justice - 4.7 Law Directory, Ministry of State Organisation - 9.5.14 Veto quorum, 9.5.15 Repeal quorum

5.2 Official channels

Through the profiles in the directories of all persons, companies, buildings and state files, the state administration is digitised. State employees who just sit in an office without doing work with citizens or work on the product are avoided. State employees enter the data in the profiles, but the official channel is now profile data and not persons or postmen.

The intranet thus offers the inexpensive and fast transmission of all necessary data between the authorities. Things like pay slips, duty rosters, orders, employment contracts, warnings are either confirmed or reported as faults by those affected.

5.3 Troubleshooting

Internal processing is handled by several algorithms and programmes that the Ministry of Digital Affairs permanently manages through its digital service. As soon as incorrect entries are noticed by state employees, they contact the internal help service of the Ministry of Digital Affairs. Faults can either be incorrect entries by state employees or faults in the programming of the algorithms. To check for incorrect entries, they are forwarded to the officials of the responsible ministry. The clerks contact the responsible state employees and check all entries together. If all the information is entered correctly, the case is either closed or handed over to the programmers if the fault is in the programming.

6 Statistical Office[25]

The Statistical Office is responsible for collecting all data collected by the state and making inventories that can be used for policy planning. The data is collected from the ministries, citizens and companies.

All information remains strictly confidential and may only be evaluated anonymously for simulation purposes. Misuse is punishable and is subject to the responsibility of the Minister

---

25 §188,1,2 Statistics: BV Art. 65, §197,3,4 Surveying: BV Art. 75a, §212,6 Structural Policy: BV Art. 103, §252,2 Metrology: BV Art. 125, §70,3 Superintendence, §71,2 Review of effectiveness.

of Digital Affairs, who may also be liable to detention together with the responsible employees due to official liability.[26]

The digital service prepares all the data as needed by the ministries and makes it available to them. On the Statistical Office's intranet site, citizens can view the data and combine them freely, similar to the way the United Nations prepares its data.[27] Citizens and companies can use the Algoracle to make forecasts and simulations based on the data. Every year, before the budget vote and after the publication of the ministries' financial plans, the statistical office prepares a forecast of the future for the coming year.[28]

6.1 Ministries

The ministries collect data on the state and development of the population, economy, society, education, research, space and environment through their work. The Ministry of Infrastructure compiles the data on the country's space, land, soil, water and air through measurements and sends the results to the Statistical Office. The office can set requirements as to what information the data must contain. The Statistical Office provides the Ministry of Labour with data on the economic and social structure of the regions and the demographic structure of the population there. This enables the Ministry of Labour to identify and promote structurally weak regions. All ministries and parties can have the Algoracle simulate individual decisions and their impact on the country as a whole.

Through the State Archives, all these data are shared with other ministries and processed by the Statistical Office. To simplify the sharing of data, the digital service standardises the collection by creating uniform templates for data collection. At the same time, in order to make the ministries' flood of data accessible to citizens, the Ministry of Digital Affairs maintains directories with profiles and groups in which the data is published, provided the owners agree. If ministries have

---

26 Ministry of Justice - 8.10.2 Data access, 8.10.3 Anonymisation
27 https://www.gapminder.org/
28 Ministry of Finance - 9 State expenditure

caused data, it belongs to the people and must be published. If citizens or companies have caused the data, ministries may use it according to applicable laws. However, citizens and companies may decide themselves on the publication of data on the intranet and grant access rights for viewing or editing.

6.2 Citizen

Citizens provide their data when they receive state services. The personal data, such as marriage, birth, illness or death, are used by the statistical office for its investigations for the Living Standard Index[29] . All voluntary data entries in the profiles of the directories are analysed, anonymised and can be used for stocktaking or simulations.

Citizens exercise oversight over the state and must therefore have unrestricted access to the anonymised static data. If they detect misconduct, they can report it to the responsible authorities. The responsible authorities are the police, the Public Prosecutor's Office and the Federal Moderator's Office. Via the profile page of the responsible state employees in the Labour Directory, citizens can send a message pointing out the misconduct.

Should anonymisation of data hinder supervision, citizens may request an opinion from the Statistical Office. A veto quorum can be raised against anonymisation. Should it be triggered, a committee[30] must decide why anonymisation is or is not permissible and submit the decider to the people for a vote.

6.3 Company

The companies provide regular data when audited by the Company Auditing Agency. All automated processes that use source code must be reported to the Company Auditing Agency. The Ministry of Digital Affairs has the right to read any source code of any programme used inland to use it for

---

29 Ministry of Finance - 10.5 Living Standard Index
30 Ministry of State Organisation - 9.6 Committee

simulation purposes. For example, source code from a CNC milling machine is used to read how fast the device can produce, when it is running unproductively, and where the load limits are. The annually updated data from the Company Auditing Agency's audits can be used to make forecasts and simulations. The companies can use the forecasts to improve their own production. They can use the simulations to estimate future market developments and adjust their production accordingly. All source codes are automatically checked for gaps during the analysis by the Algoracle and reported to the author of the source code in order to be able to close the gaps. After the gaps have been closed, the source code is newly checked. This service is provided by the technical auditors of the Company Auditing Agency. Source codes that have been checked without any gaps being found receive a certificate from the Company Auditing Agency.

7 Digital data protection[31]

Everyone who owns and uses data is obliged to protect it. Data protection means preventing access by unauthorised persons and using the data only for the purpose agreed with the owner. Data must also be protected against misappropriation or manipulation. The purpose for which state employees can use data is regularised by law.
Data protection law extends from administrative law to consumer policy in the information society. State administration is administered via the intranet to ensure data protection.

7.1 Private data protection

Private data protection on the Internet is the responsibility of the persons and companies themselves and they must abide by their mutual contractual terms. Consumers can use the intranet and the internet for their digital relationships. Data sovereignty remains with the originator and thus owner of the

---

31 §10 Protection of privacy: BV Art.13, §14 Data protection: KV Art.18, §41,5 Exercise of political rights: BV Art.39, §207,3,7 Telecommunications, §113,7 Media democracy

data in both networks. Digital customer relationships are only protected by the state on the intranet and not on the internet. Data protection on the Internet is limited to the prevention and prosecution of criminal offences. Private data protection means the use of programmes for encryption and prevention of danger that companies offer to consumers.

Data protection also includes the secrecy of correspondence. Accordingly, broadcasts may only be opened if there is reasonable suspicion of a criminal offence and may never be altered. In order to integrate the analogue secrecy of correspondence into digital data protection, the envelope around a letter or the package of a broadcast, corresponds to encryption.

7.2 State data protection

The Ministry of Digital Affairs is responsible for data protection on the intranet. Data protection on the intranet is guaranteed for citizens, companies and ministries by networks, hardware and software from the People's Innovation Company intranet. Data that serve the purpose of political participation are specially protected. This special protection is ensured by the fact that voting on constitutional articles, politicians and laws can only be carried out at the town halls' voting computers. Votes for quorums can be cast via the People's Computer, but once the quorum is triggered and voting takes place, all voters are asked to indicate whether they have actually cast their vote for the relevant quorum. Data queries via the Algoracle can only be made on computers on the intranet.

Data protection on the intranet also refers to the authenticity and accuracy of the data. Because the use of the intranet requires an identity check at the beginning of each use, all users are on the intranet with their clear name and can conclude notarised treaties or prove their eligibility to vote for quorums, ratings, contributions and comments.

State data protection means encrypting sent data using quantum cryptography and securing networks, storage locations and operating systems. When state data carriers are attacked, a counter-attack is automatically carried out.

State data protection is automatically granted to all users of the intranet. This level of protection is democratically agreed and democratically confirmed and controlled through voting and personnel. All data belongs to the citizens personally and represents a property value. All data is shared with the state because citizens can deselect the responsible politicians in case of misuse. Every act on the intranet can be traced back to a responsible person. Whoever had an idea first can be traced. Multiple voting and pseudonyms are prevented. Administrators and group leaders are elected by all affected users in a digital election of persons. Crimes can be automatically reported via a police call button.

The Company Auditing Agency's technical auditors regularly inspect the facilities where the Intranet's servers and networks are stored. The inspection work is filmed at random by Surveillance Television .[32]

7.3 Storage locations[33]

All personal data is stored on a citizen's People's Computer. The owner can view all data stored on his People's Computer. The data is encrypted and transferred to a high-security server once a month as a backup copy. Every month, all newly added data is transferred from the People's Computers to the high-security server. These copies serve as backups for the citizens in case People's Computers are broken or lost. Anyone who breaks or loses their People's Computer must add all the lost data from the previous month to the new People's Computer. Anyone who loses their People's Computer must report it immediately to the police so that it can be located, found or destroyed.

All data that the state collects on the citizen should be available digitally to be stored in the People's Computer of the affected citizen. All ministries, except the Ministry of Security, that create files on a citizen must maintain and store these files in the citizen's People's Computer. State agencies immediately back up this data to the high-security server of the Ministry of

---

32Ministry of Media - 12 Surveillance Television
33§13.5 Freedom of expression and information: KV Art.17

Digital Affairs. Access to the data on this high-security server is for user data recovery and law enforcement, but not for any other state use.

7.3.1 Server

To ensure fast availability, data processing servers are distributed throughout the country. Private data is located on the People's Computers and stored redundantly on 3 special high-security servers at different locations in the country. The Ministry of Digital Affairs has several known and secured bunkers where the intranet data processing servers are located. In the capital city of the Ministry of Digital Affairs there is one and in another secure known location inland, there are two high security servers. Each individual high-security server contains the data of all People's Computers. The network engineers decide on the server locations for data processing, which contain the data of all users that are not stored in the People's Computer. The locations are always known and secured.

Only the Ministry of Security is allowed to access the high-security server for criminal investigations, all other ministries have to access the data via the People's Computers. The Ministry of Justice monitors all accesses and checks whether they are lawful as soon as charges are brought. As soon as a case is closed, the accesses must be entered in the Access Directory in the People's Computer of all affected citizens.

The high-security server is never connected directly to the intranet, but is only supported with data via an external data carrier without its own operating system. It has its own power supply and no WLAN or other Internet connection. Backup DVDs or newer data carriers that last a long time are created every year. As soon as a person has died, their data is transferred to the high-security server and then deleted from the People's Computer. In the case of genealogical research, individual profiles are released for viewing, which a citizen can also dispose of in his or her will. 100 years after a citizen's death, all data that was once on the People's Computer is released.

The data security of the servers is guaranteed by structural and technical measures. Data integrity and protection of personal data is ensured by the People's Computers and the Access Directory. Availability and security of the data should be balanced, which is ensured by the People's Innovation Company Intranet. The Minister of Digital Affairs ensures that the servers are economically utilised and advertises for sufficient tax funds in the annual budget vote.

7.3.2 Networks

The transmission masts and cables are set up by the Ministry of Infrastructure.[34] The Ministry of Digital Affairs administers this infrastructure with the necessary operating software and is responsible for the smooth contact of the users. All transmission masts and cables must be monitored and secured so that foreign manipulation can be excluded. The use of the networks, except for the intranet network, is subject to a charge.

7.4 Access rights[35]

Different persons have different rights to enter data about the same person. State employees can enter data about a person that is required by law, such as the information on the identity card. The person cannot change this information, even though he or she owns it. What the person is allowed to do, however, is to limit the viewing rights to a certain group of persons. The group of persons must include at least all employees of the state who are authorised to do so by law.

A person may enter data about him/herself. This may be voluntary or by law or under a treaty with another person. Other persons have no right to change this information. The owner grants the right to view to a group of persons chosen by the owner. If data entry is required by law, responsible state employees have the right to view the data.

34Ministry of Infrastructure - 6.2.3 Data network, 5.3.3 Networks and transport routes
35§10 Protection of privacy: BV Art.13

Persons can contractually grant each other the right to enter data about each other and distribute viewing and writing rights. Data owners have the right to delete or have deleted their data as long as the data is not required by law.

The people determine which data are required by law through their consent to a corresponding law or in a committee. Which data is necessary for cooperation is determined by the contracting parties. Which data owners wish to disclose voluntarily is left up to them. Access to data by the state, including in law enforcement, must be bound by law.

7.4.1 Share data

Citizens may only access the data of other citizens if the affected citizens have allowed this in advance via their own People's Computer. Each citizen may decide for himself/herself which data he/she publishes for certain contact persons, economic forms or companies and whether this group of persons may also pass on the data to third parties.

7.4.2 State access

The general rule is that state agencies may access all data, but this must be noted immediately in the access log on the home page of the Access Directory. State agencies may only publish the data anonymously. Thus, at least the first and last name must be deleted. If the radius of publication is small, the address is also anonymised, making it impossible to draw conclusions about a specific person.

Personal data that users have not publicly released themselves always require a legal basis for state access. The appropriate paragraph is stored in the access log for the respective entry. In this way, citizens can vote directly against the law if they do not agree with it. If the repeal quorum is reached, the law must either be abolished or adapted by the digital minister.

7.4.2.1 Disclosure

In policy work, it is always the minister who decides on the access of his ministry to the data on the intranet. The employees of the ministry who have access to this data are bound to secrecy and are only authorised to transmit the data to the state employees authorised by law. They are never authorised to disclose the data to third parties, i.e. state employees who have nothing to do with the case or persons outside the state service.

7.5 Access Directory[36]

The Access Directory stores all accesses to data carriers that are connected to the intranet. It can only be viewed without restriction by the Ministry of Digital Affairs. All other users are only granted viewing rights for retrievals and accesses to their own data carriers.
All citizens' data are stored in the People's Computer of the respective citizen, all data of the state are stored in the State Archives. Retrieval is defined as the transfer of data from another data carrier to one's own data carrier. Access is when one's own data is transferred to another data carrier.

7.5.1 Access logs

All accesses to all data of a citizen are stored in the Access Directory in the People's Computer of this citizen in So-called access logs. This includes own, state, friendly or corporate accesses. In the case of secret data retrieval in preliminary investigations, the data retrieval is only entered once the preliminary investigation has ended. All newly created access logs are marked as "new" and printed in bold. One can display all accesses sorted by date, ministry or alphabetically, similar to an email inbox.

36§14,4 Data protection: KV Art.18

7.5.2 Private access

Citizens learn from the access logs why data was accessed and by whom, what the purpose was and to whom else the data was sent. Links to the profiles of the persons who accessed the data are created in the access log.
The owner of the data can then deny or allow future access. For this purpose, each Access Directory offers its user choices in the security settings.

7.5.3 State accesses

Citizens can track every state access and see the purpose of use and the basis of the law. If you still consider an access to be unlawful, you can either reject the law by means of a repeal quorum or report a suspected data misuse to the police. Any access can be authorised by doing nothing or by ticking "why?" or "I don't want that".
The tick "why?" shows the purpose for which the data was retrieved. This includes the official channel, which state employees had access to this data as well as the paragraph for the legal authorisation to retrieve the data. If you tick the box "I don't want that!", you are automatically redirected to the text of the law and can reject the law by casting your vote in the repeal quorum. In the case of the security agencies, for investigative tactical reasons, the accesses are only disclosed after conviction or case closure.

7.5.4 Profiles for data carriers

Each data carrier is given a profile in the Access Directory. The profile shows who owns the data carrier. If a data carrier retrieves data from another data carrier, this process is saved on both profiles. All access logs are listed as posts on the profile's pin board according to retrieval, access, date, reason or user.
A data carrier can belong to a person, such as a People's Computer. Then this person can see all foreign accesses to his or her data carrier in the profile as well as his or her own retrievals from foreign data carriers. These viewing rights

make it possible to check the retrievals and accesses.

7.5.5 Groups for owners

A data carrier can belong to several persons, such as a computer or server of a company. These persons form a group and can assign one person to check the profile.
A data carrier can also belong to the citizens of a municipality or to the people. This is the case with all data carriers used by the state. All state data carriers can be accessed via the state archives and belong to a ministry or a specific agency of a ministry. Every ministry whose data has been accessed and every ministry that has accessed data is listed here as an access log and is publicly accessible. This does not include access logs of ongoing preliminary investigations. Citizens auditing accesses to or from ministries can form audit groups to share ministries and departments.

8 Digital crime

The Ministry of Security maintains a digital police force and a digital warfare army.[37] The police investigate data misuse and unauthorised access to data. Either users report the misuse or theft of data or the police come across breaches during investigations. The military's digital defence service is able to send counterattacks to the right addressees. The communication of the security agencies involved runs via an independent secured radio network for all authorities and organisations with security tasks.

8.1 Institute for Information Security

The Ministry of Digital Affairs, in cooperation with the Ministries of Security and Education, operates an Institute for Information Security to defend against and combat cybercrime. In this institute, gaps in systems are searched for, weak points are detected and weapons such as viruses, Trojans or worms are developed. Developers and programmers from

---

37 Ministry of Security - 7.7 Digital Police, 9.5.1 Digital Warfare

the People's Innovation Company Intranet, teachers and researchers from the computer science subject area at the colleges and universities, as well as police and army personnel work at the institute.

8.2 Cyber defence

Cyber defence aims to prevent strangers from accessing the intranet or impersonating another person. The servers that administer the network of People's Computers recognise users and encrypt data. The constant encryption of all data and communication is to prevent eavesdropping or manipulation. A security programme continuously checks all activities on the intranet and reports to the police any anomalies or deviations from the usual user behaviour.

The operating system of these servers has several built-in viruses that are constantly looking for a host. As soon as an unregistered device is connected to the intranet, the viruses are immediately transmitted and attack the foreign device. They are designed to render the affected device unusable. These viruses are developed by the Ministry of Security. The army provides its obsolete cyber defence weapons.

The Institute for Information Security, in voting with the police, supports ministries whose digital administration has been attacked, eliminates gaps and carries out counterattacks with current digital weapon systems of the army. If citizens or companies on the intranet have become victims of digital crime, they receive the same support as ministries, but only outdated army weapon systems are used for counterattack.

9 Digital economy

The digital economy includes services related to Information Technology, telecommunications, media and postal services. In a national and continental agenda, fundamental ethical, regulatory and competition policy issues are continuously raised by politicians, entrepreneurs and consumers and clarified with the digital minister, if necessary in a committee. The agenda adapts to the current state of technology.

Currently, the development of artificial intelligence and the data economy are being put to the test as to how far they can serve the common good and provide for technical progress to raise living standards. The communitarisation of the intranet is being promoted in the international digital dialogue and the demarcation from the internet is being maintained. E-government should only be possible via the intranet. Intranet governance is the responsibility of the Ministry of Digital Affairs. Internet governance can only be taken over by the Ministry of Digital Affairs once all states have united to form the united states of the world. Until then, the internet remains a free space that cannot be entirely controlled by the state. However, in order to prevent criminal offences, areas of the internet in the country can be blocked or sections censored. Blocking or censorship must be reported to the user and justified by law.

The digital economy is promoted to different degrees depending on the economic form in which a company is registered. This can range from simply registering the company in the Labour Directory and using the People's Bank tax account to the entire digital administration of a company, including the necessary information technology from the People's Innovation Company intranet.

If companies decide to use the intranet, they have to share their data with the state for simulation purposes. They receive benefits for this, but have to pay for the services.

Companies that decide to operate their information technology via the Internet must take the necessary precautions themselves.

9.1 Digital notary

Data and treaties that should not be able to be manipulated subsequently can be stored on the server of the Ministry of Digital Affairs. All parties to the treaty save a copy of the treaty and a copy is saved on the security server and sent to all participants involved in the event of a dispute. Data involving industrial property rights are stored and opened in court proceedings to clarify legal and liability claims.

9.2 Companies of the economic forms

The ministries of economy are allowed to use all company data to keep their economy stable or to be able to achieve a growth target. For business consultancy purposes, the Company Auditing Agency's business consultants may use anonymised company data if one of the following three conditions is met. This is the case if, firstly, the company being advised is making losses and jobs are at risk, secondly, the industry association identifies a shortage or an excessive price, and thirdly, if the companies agree to the disclosure of their data. Companies participating in the success model programme[38] agree to share their data in order to share the most efficient work processes and develop them together.

Barter economy companies can offer their goods and services on their profile pages in the Labour Directory, but they do not have to. In the same way, consumers can indicate their demand and their means of exchange in the intranet swap shop, but they do not have to do so.

Planned Economy enterprises need to document and organise all their work processes and record keeping on the intranet on the company's profile page in the Labour Directory. This enables all companies in the planning network to react to current and future demand at an early stage. In the planning network, the principle applies: whoever provides all his data may also access all other given data. This means that an oversupply or shortage can be recognised and adjusted at an early stage. Demanders communicate their consumption by presenting their social village card. Similar to the Payback card[39] , all customer data is recorded here and transmitted to the planning network of the companies that offer this good or service. In the Planned Economy, citizens gain admission to the economic data of the companies and customers.[40]

The companies of the Social Market Economy have to publish the economic data of the audit report after the audit by the Company Auditing Agency, which joint-stock companies of

---

38 Ministry of Social Market Economy - 17.2.1 Success model programme
39 https://www.payback.de/
40 Ministry of Planned Economy - 4.7 Social card, 7.3 Needs assessment

the Free Market Economy also have to publish. In addition, they also publish the satisfaction of their employees, which was asked in the Company Auditing Agency's surveys.

The companies in the Free Market Economy are almost not required to publish any data. Joint-stock companies are obliged to publish data that investors specify. Other companies in the Free Market Economy are only required to have a profile in the Labour Directory and to publish all their advertised jobs there. As their tax levies are linked to their turnover, the company account movements are managed through the tax account at People's Bank.[41] Depending on how much data they publish themselves, the prices for simulations decrease.

10 Internet

The Ministry of Digital Affairs ensures that domestic laws are applied to parts of the internet that are used domestically. For this purpose, the Digital Police operates a page on the Internet through which complaints can be filed. To file a digital complaint, the internet address must be pasted or forwarded via email. Via a companion application for internet browsers, users can document virtual crimes and alert the police. The companion application is designed to catch offenders in the act and preserve evidence.[42]

10.1 Free intranet

The free intranet is a website through which all the open source software of the People's Innovation Company Intranet is made available as a Linux version for free download. This source code is also public. This should firstly make it possible to spread the dynamic media democracy in a guerrilla tactic without the state first having to build an intranet. All applications of the voting computers and People's Computers can thus also be installed on conventional devices. Although data security is then lower, the initial democratic self-organisation of citizens and companies is easier. Secondly, the open source software of

---

41 Ministry of Finance - 11.6 Corporate Account
42 Ministry of Security - 7.7.1 Internet

the worldwide open source community makes it possible to find damage or security gaps in the programmes and operating systems and to programme improvements. The security gaps can then also be checked in the intranet version and fixed if necessary.

10.2 Interfaces

Certain data from the Internet should not have to be newly entered into the People's Computer, but should be able to be imported. This should be possible, for example, with Wikipedia and the Knowledge Directory. For the import, a request is made to the digital service. The data is transferred to the intranet via a server of the Ministry of Digital Affairs. For data security, only texts, videos and images from the internet can be imported that have previously been checked by the Ministry of Digital Affairs. The source code of the analysis programmes is open. Competitions are held in which prizes are offered to outsmart the programme.

10.2.1 Knowledge.dir[43]

The Knowledge Directory is exported monthly from the servers and published on the Internet on the Knowledge.dir website of the Ministry of Digital Affairs. The authors of the contributions in the intranet-based Knowledge Directory can decide for themselves whether they agree to publication on the Internet. All persons depicted in pictures and sound must also give their consent in writing before publication. To do this, a request is sent to their People's Computer. The algorithm determines all the participants involved through user behaviour, facial and voice recognition. Each person identified is asked whether he or she is the person depicted or heard. If a user confirms his or her identity in the post, he or she is asked whether the post may be published on the internet. If more than one user confirms the same identity, a face-to-face verification must take place, which includes a

---

43§182.2 Further education: BV Art. 64a

video call between a member of the digital service staff and the identified persons.

11 Intranet[44]

The intranet provides for a digital society that uses the information technology of the People's Innovation Company Intranet to organise itself in a self-determined manner. The Ministry of Digital Affairs pursues the digital strategy of decentralising data and decision-makers, but at the same time allowing any number of people to gather at any time to vote together on decisions. Fundamental questions of the information society are discussed democratically by the user community and decisions concerning the intranet are made in voting with the digital minister. All those entitled to vote can participate directly in political processes via the intranet, in accordance with their political rights. The intranet is subject to state data protection.

The intranet is a highly legal place because all users have to register with their identity card and all actions can be traced back to them personally. Anonymity can be cared for by citizens on the internet or in public, where they do not have to constantly expel themselves. Security-relevant data, such as satellite images of defence installations, simulations with an investigative background or data classified as confidential or secret, cannot be accessed on the intranet. Users receive an appropriate explanation if they are denied access.

11.1 Intranet café[45]

There is an intranet café in every town hall.[46] There, citizens can go to the intranet, get all the services and products of the People's Innovation Company Intranet and vote in the voting booths. The intranet café also serves as the first point of contact in the town hall and as a waiting area. It is open 24

44§41,2,5 Exercise of political rights: BV Art.39, §94 Digital participation in committees, §207,4 Telecommunications
45Ministry of State Organisation - 8.2.1 Intranet Café
46Ministry of State Organisation - 8.2.1.1 Election week, 8.2.1.2 Polling booths

hours a day, 7 days a week and the information desk is always manned. Workers from the Ministry of Digital Affairs work in the intranet café in shifts and also use it as their office in the town hall. The intranet café consists of a counter, lockers, tables with partitions, computers and chairs.

At the counter, People's Innovation Company Intranet devices can be purchased, exchanged or sent for repair and picked up again. Exchange devices are always in stock. Via the computer at the counter, the staff member can retrieve the last backup copy of the citizen's old People's Computer from the high-security server and save it on the replacement device. The same computer is also used for the initial registration of new users of the intranet and to make the identity card capable of logging on to the intranet. Additional devices for the People's Computer, such as the Virtual Reality glasses, can also be lent out and returned at the counter.

In the lockers, data carriers are stored by citizens who do not want to use a People's Computer. The citizens can connect the data carriers in the locker to the intranet in order to access them via a computer in the intranet café. Once the data carrier is connected to the locker, citizens can access it from any Intranet café. When moving, citizens take their data carrier with them to the town hall of their new place of residence.

The majority of the intranet café consists of individually separated computer workstations with tables and chairs. There, citizens can surf the intranet free of charge for as long as they like. As soon as one logs in with one's identity card, the servers are accessed and the internal memory of one's People's Computer. The user interface of the computers in the Intranet Café is identical to that of all People's Computers. On all computers of the Intranet Café and all People's Computers, the citizen is greeted by the same start page, menu navigation, operation, existing personal data and all entries made so far on the Intranet. All input options are the same on all operating elements of the intranet, except in the case of security-relevant applications.

Certain applications or search queries can only be made from a computer in the Intranet Café. For example, searches from the Algoracle can only be made in the intranet café. The results are then sent to the People's Computer so that no single People's Computer can access the entire intranet database.

The area with the computer workstations also serves as a waiting area for the town hall. Anyone who has to wait for a member of staff in the town hall is given a radio sensor that alerts them when it is their turn. The radio sensor is handed out and returned at the counter.

There are permanent voting booths in the intranet café where people can vote during the election weeks.[47]

11.2 Intranet address

The intranet address is composed as follows. It starts with "in", which stands for "intranet". This is followed by a dot and the name of the page. If the page is in a directory, the name is followed by a dot and "dir" for directory. The storage path on the server is indicated by the names of the folders, which are separated by /.

If the intranet address is the reference to the virtual map of the country, the page is named like the name of the country and instead of the folder path, the coordinates and the viewing height are given and separated by /.

11.3 Admission[48]

Admission to the intranet is either via the People's Computer or in the intranet café. Access authorisation is granted to all nationals from the age of ten. Foreigners growing up inland receive access authorisation from the age of ten until the age of majority. Naturalised persons receive access entitlement from the age of majority. The identity card is required for admission.[49] Depending on the type of identity card, there are different access authorisations.

Until the age of majority, children only have writing and voting rights for the Ministry of Family Affairs and the

[47] §84,1,2,3,4,8 Political civil rights
[48] Ministry of Integration - 4.4.1 Identity cards
[49] Ministry of Justice - 7.5.1 Restriction of Rights, Ministry of Education - 12.4 Digitalised Education

Ministry of Education. Profiles can only be created in the Persons Directory, Family Directory and Education Directory. Otherwise, all pages and directories are open for viewing.

Naturalised persons do not have write-in and voting rights for legislative procedures and the election of politicians. However, voting is permitted for statistical purposes in order to record differences and similarities in voting behaviour.

For nationals, there are no restrictions from the age of majority until death.

Should legislative processes or elections of persons take place at the municipal level, only citizens residing in that municipality are granted the corresponding admission. Should political processes take place at the international level, those nationals of the affected states are also entitled to vote. If their state does not have an intranet, they can log on to the internet via the free intranet and participate in the digital opportunities for democratic co-determination. The Ministry of Digital Affairs ensures a timely feed of the foreigners' data from the internet into the intranet.

Citizens who are in detention are not given admission to the intranet, except for the digitalised education areas.

11.3.1 Admission procedure

Activation is the same for all People's Computers and computers in the Intranet Café. First, the identity card must be expelled into the slot on the device. Now you enter the eight-digit PIN number you have set yourself. The default setting is the date of birth. Now you have to hold your guide eye about 10 cm in front of the camera on the device. There is an LED light around the lens. As soon as the eye is positioned correctly, the light comes on. If the shot is successful, the entire screen turns green for two seconds. The last process is the fingerprint, which simultaneously confirms that you have control over this device from now on. The start page of the operating system opens. The device can now be operated.

11.4 People's Navigator

The People's Navigator serves to connect the virtual world of the intranet with the real world in the country. The user enters the intranet via the People's Navigator. It is the only browser for the intranet with special encryption. The user can set privacy settings for all pages and directories of the intranet, set a start page, search pages, create bookmarks, alert the police, photograph the screen or make a screen video. Other additional applications for the browser can be created by voluntary users themselves because the source code is open.

11.4.1 Translation: Virtual World - Real World

Citizens can conduct policy negotiations in the virtual world for implementation in the real world. Legislative initiatives by citizens or legislative proposals by the government can be discussed and voted on. All registered political meetings are automatically displayed in the virtual domestic. Thus, all citizens nationwide can participate in the voting held at these events. However, if only municipal and not national groups of persons are affected, only citizens within the affected radius of the postcode are entitled to vote. The decisive final votes only take place in the real world, namely during an election week on the voting computer in the polling booth in the town hall. The intranet also maps economic reality virtually. Companies that have a domestic location are shown on the map of the virtual inland at the corresponding location. Clicking on the company automatically opens the link to the company's profile in the Labour Directory. Users can obtain information about the company or order goods and services. For this purpose, the company's profile in the Labour Directory is supplemented by a web shop free of charge. The webshop can be accessed via the virtual map or via the Labour Directory. For orders, the identity card must also be a People's Bank account card. Shipping only works within the country.

11.4.2 Translation: Real World - Virtual World

The environment in the virtual world corresponds to three-dimensional satellite images of the country. Machines and persons move as the Statistical Office data predicts, as long as they are not moved by their users themselves. Every holder of a domestic identity card automatically gets a profile in the Persons Directory and an avatar in the virtual inland. The user can do things with his avatar in the virtual domestic. If one does nothing, the avatar is automatically moved according to the forecasts of the Statistical Office. The personal data, such as name, date of birth, place of birth, height and address, are by default invisible to all other users. Only the user himself can release his data to the intranet at any time and also undo it. All his statements are retained and remain visible to all those to whom he grants admission to his data.
Users can virtually use rooms and places that have been virtualised. They can talk and trade with each other. All means of public transport virtually adhere to real timetables.

11.4.3 Page layout

The page structure of the People's Navigator is always similar. The pages, top, bottom, right and left are control panels that can be faded in and out. When fading in, only a part can extend into the central panel or be displayed as a full screen.

11.4.3.1 Top: Control commands

Control commands can be used to move the view or your own avatar across the playing field. In the upper bar, all control commands can be entered that can also be executed with the mouse, keyboard or gestures on a touch screen. The keyboard shortcuts and gestures are displayed when you move the mouse pointer or your finger over the corresponding field. Depending on the perspective in which the playing field is operated, the control options change. You can scroll from the orbital view to the first-person perspective. You can move through the playing field as a spectator or send your avatar on a virtual journey.

11.4.3.2 Left: Search

The search function is designed to help you find responsible ministries more quickly in order to access state services. There is a search bar at the top left. If you enter something here, all pages and directories of the intranet are searched and listed as results below. If you want to narrow down the search results, you will find a selection field for ministries, directories, programmes or the most recent date below the search bar. If content can be assigned to a ministry, it is marked with coloured squares whose colour corresponds to that of the respective ministry.

If the left-hand side is transferred to full screen, all search results are displayed one below the other and the responsibility of the ministries is shown as paths next to each. The path extends from the headquarters of the ministry to the municipal office of a department. If you click on the path, the path is shown in colour in the ministry's organigram.

The field "Advanced search settings" can be used to narrow down the search results according to responsibility or a certain group of persons, for example, in the circle of acquaintances of the Persons Directory, in the vicinity of a postcode or a certain location, a subject area of a college or a branch of industry for companies. For each setting, a tick can be set so that this search filter is activated. In this way, several search filters can be activated at the same time.

11.4.3.3 Right: Latest reports

Here, the latest reports are displayed, which the user sets himself. You can enter your interests and follow specific groups. If voting is pending, the remaining time is displayed. Depending on which ministry one is interested in, one selects its homepage, logs in with one's profile from the Persons Directory and can join all shared groups and leave posts, comments or ratings on noticeboards. You can also follow a group just to follow the chat without writing privileges and participate in voting and opinion polls that the group members ask their viewers.

Each post in a group contains a headline and a picture or video that illustrates the topic of the chat. The reports can be sorted into newest, most popular, new and popular. For each group that you follow or join, you can mark interesting posts as "interesting" by ticking them. You will then receive the latest reports from this group.

Ministries can also be followed. Then one gets admission to all activity reports, but can narrow down the selection by means of the organigram. In addition, one has the possibility to take a look at all legislative processes that are currently being worked on in this ministry. If you are interested in participating in the process, you will find a link for this legislative project in the Legislative Directory[50] .

The full screen display shows a mind map of all the latest reports that affect you, a specific group or a group of persons.

11.4.3.4 Below: Display field

The display field shows all the information about what you have clicked on in the field. If you have clicked on something that has an intranet page or a profile page in a directory, the page is displayed here. The page continues down into the edge of the screen and can be viewed in sections by scrolling. To enlarge the section of the screen, the bottom bar can be displayed as a full screen.

11.4.3.5 Central: Playing field

The playing field is a map of the virtually recreated inland. Three-dimensional satellite images are used to model the landscape, including buildings and moving parts. The satellite images consist of videos so that movements can be recognised and virtually recreated. Animals and humans are recognised with infrared cameras. Humans are linked to their profile in

---

50 Ministry of State Organisation - 9.10.6.1 Legislative Directory

the Persons Directory, foreigners to their passport, which was scanned upon entry. Anyone who owns a People's Computer automatically receives an avatar that virtually represents the real human.

11.4.3.5.1 Navigation

As soon as you move the mouse pointer over the map, you can click on it and move it in all directions. If you scroll forward with the mouse wheel, the satellite view moves closer and closer to the ground. As soon as you have reached the viewing height of five metres, the camera swings from the bird's eye view to the first-person view. The operation has now changed from a strategy game to a first-person shooter. One's own avatar then appears in front of one on the screen and can be moved forwards, backwards, to the right or to the left by using the arrow keys on the keyboard. As soon as you open the People's Navigator, you see your own avatar on the playing field in the place where your People's Computer is located.

11.4.3.5.2 Simulation of the real time

The inland is completely recreated virtually with all the data available on the intranet. For simulation purposes, all data is evaluated and displayed as an anonymised result. The real state of the country is simulated in real time.
Especially traffic data of means of transport, money, goods and crowds are important for the simulation. For this purpose, all source codes of programmes and their data are incorporated into the algorithm for the simulation. This ranges from the operating software of a cash register and the data of all cash registers located inland, to the computer programme for high-frequency trading and its data on purchases and sales. All interpersonal transactions recorded via electronic media also flow into the intranet data set. For state users who are authorised by law, all data is displayed. For private users, citizens can hide their data or only release it to individual persons.

As soon as a user reduces the perimeter of his simulation in such a way that he can view the behaviour of his family, friends or colleagues, all participants receive a search request via their Access Directory indicating the purpose of the simulation. They can accept or reject the request. If they reject it, their data is not included in the simulation.

11.4.3.5.3 Simulation of the future

A date function can be used to simulate a fast forward to a self-selected date. These future simulations are a service of the computer programme Algoracle. The current data set of the intranet is used to predict the future. The more users participate, the better the predictions become. For each prediction, the programme shows how many persons have participated and how high the probability of deviations could be.

11.4.4 Avatars

Avatars are virtual three-dimensional images of the user data. They move around the three-dimensional map of the inland and can enter buildings that have been made accessible with the indoor virtualiser. The avatars automatically do what has been entered in the users' profiles. If the avatar itself is actively operated by the user, it is displayed brighter.

11.4.4.1 Avatar appearance

Basically, the avatar is of human shape and is based on the user's appearance. The colour of the skin, hair, eyes, height and gender correspond to the information on the user's identity card. Weight and body stature correspond to the information on the Health Card. Avatars of underage users are represented by the shaded coloured dot below them.
The face is modelled by the three-dimensional ID image[51] .
At domestic airports with body scanners, users are allowed to

---

51 Ministry of Integration - 4.4.1 Identity cards

have this data sent to their People's Computer to form their avatar.

11.4.4.2 Visibility of the avatar

The user sees all other avatars in his or her vicinity who have switched on their visibility and whom the user would also like to have displayed. Lists can be created for each directory to mark their own contacts. In this way, different group members can be selected from the directories or friend and work groups can be created whose members are then displayed on the map. Users can also make themselves visible only to certain other users. There is a selection menu for this purpose. Users can choose to show no profiles, only certain profiles, or all the profiles they have in the various directories. Every citizen has a profile in the Persons Directory, as a pupil also in the Education Directory and as a worker also in the Labour Directory. New entries of a person in a directory are automatically synchronised. However, their visibility on the profile view must be approved by the user for each directory individually. In the selection menu, it is possible to create a list of which entries from which directories should be made visible to which groups of persons in the future.

11.4.4.3 Possible actions of the avatar

Users can use their avatars to perform various acts on the intranet. These include legally binding transactions of capital and labour as well as notarised treaties.

11.4.4.3.1 Play or work

With the avatar, you can walk, drive or fly through the virtual inland. The current means of transport are to be used for this. Actions of the avatar basically run in real time so that the use is designed like in a computer game or browser game. However, if you do not want to play a game, but want to get to your destination as quickly as possible because you have a purpose, you move over the map with the mouse pointer and not with the avatar. This function is activated or deactivated in the upper bar. If the work function is activated, it is possible to click on all the virtually represented citizens, companies and state agencies and to work with them with effects on the real life of the user and not the avatar.

11.4.4.3.2 Buy and sell

All buildings that offer goods or services inland can be reached via the map. To find buildings, you can either search for the address using the search function or move the mouse pointer to the location on the map and scroll as close as possible. If you take the address from the search, you jump directly there. All suppliers of goods and services have the option of scanning their premises via the indoor virtualiser and sending it to the Ministry of Digital Affairs. All available goods can be scanned with the barcode and thus represent a virtual inventory list that is linked to the cash register and thus automatically shows entrepreneurs the current stock. Employees on duty can also be entered into this system and receive a barcode with their working hours, current orders, wages and training. Companies can use it to digitalise their entire administration, recruitment, purchasing and sales. With free admission to the Labour Directory, all domestic companies and citizens can trade goods, services and labour. Payments are made online via People's Bank. Goods are delivered by parcel service or service providers come to the agreed meeting point. Voluntary sellers can also offer their goods and services virtually for an avatar. The suppliers decide whether this virtual service should also be paid for or used as advertising.

11.4.4.3.3 Visit and communicate

Users can communicate either through their messaging service in the Persons Directory or through their avatars. Users can exchange data instantly via the messaging service, create news in text, image, sound or video, make phone calls or video calls.

Avatars must meet in order to converse. Avatars can either be automatically controlled or directly managed by the user. Communication via live chat, telephony or video telephony is only possible with directly controlled avatars, not with automatically controlled avatars. Automatically controlled avatars can leave a message for the user.

You can click on any avatar that is in the environment of your own avatar. This opens a chat window that is visible to all those who are also in the same environment. Each additional avatar of another user has the possibility to join in and talk by clicking on the text field. For private chats, people arrange to meet in their living room or workplace.

The visible communication of the avatars is done with their hands. They do the sign language while they speak. The sound while speaking is either the real voice of the user or a computer voice that reads out what the user writes. Everything spoken is automatically converted into text form so that information, arguments or ideas can be looked up more quickly later. The sending user can decide whether to speak or write. For receiving users, both variants are always available.

If you want to contact a user, you can use the avatar or the mouse pointer to move to the place where you think that person lives, works or is suspected of living, or you can use the search. If the avatar's user is online, one can click on him or her to talk. If the avatar is managed automatically or if the user does not have time at the moment, a message can be left in the letterbox. To do this, click on the letterbox on the avatar's building so that a message window appears. Once the news has been written, click on "deliver". The message now appears in the recipient's mailbox in the news service.

11.4.4.3.4 Discuss and vote

Anyone who wants to participate in the policy process must go virtually with their avatar to the location of the committee or to the capital city of the appropriate ministry in the premises of the responsible party. Here, initiatives and negotiation processes for laws take place permanently in the rooms and council buildings of the party headquarters.

Any user may permanently participate in the ongoing procedures for government decisions and laws. This can happen through a text, a picture, a video or an audio recording. All ongoing committees that affect the whole country are displayed and the avatars can participate virtually everywhere. In virtual participation, the camera image from the event is transmitted to the intranet and simulated. Simulated citizens participating in the real event are shown virtually only pale or as stick figures. Avatars can stand there and are shown normally. At public events, avatars also have the right to speak and can register with the moderator to speak. Their contribution is then made via video telephony. If users want to move their avatars to the places of action immediately and not in real time, they can play policy manager and teleport their avatar.

11.4.5 Select directory

The People's Navigator gives the user an overview of all directories and how active the user is in them. All directories can be selected via the left control panel. For the user's personal overview, all his or her profile pages from directories are displayed, as well as his or her network with other profiles and groups and how much contact is maintained with these profiles or groups. If all settings from the search are retained and the left control panel is folded in, only the avatars or buildings of the selected directories, profiles and groups are displayed or marked in colour on the map.

11.4.5.1 Register

In the left-hand control panel for the search, you can click directly on "Directories" without using the search. Then a tab is displayed on the left side below, in which all ministries are listed one below the other. There is a cross to the left of the ministry name. If you click on it, all its directories are displayed under the ministry. There is also a cross next to it; if you click on it, "Profiles", "Groups" and "Categories" are displayed under the directory. If you click on one of the three or on the names of the ministries or directories, the corresponding contents are displayed in full screen mode.

11.4.5.2 Tree structure

If you use the search, all results are displayed in a tree structure. The path is structured as follows. Directory - Group / Profile - Pinboard - Post / Comment / Rating
Any number of groups or profiles can originate from the directory, and any number of posts, comments or ratings can originate from their pin boards. The end of all paths can be displayed as a list. Using the upper control panel, the search results can be sorted according to certain categories.

11.4.5.3 Circle view

The overview of the profile pages is displayed in a circular arrangement of all profile pages in small format, which can be rotated by the user like a carousel. The profile page in the foreground can be clicked on and is displayed in full screen.

11.4.5.4 Pie chart

The network of a user is displayed as a pie chart. The user is in the centre. Around him are points close to or far from him. The closer a point is to the centre, the stronger the contact to this profile or group. Each pie slice represents a directory. The larger the pie slice, the more frequent the contact with more profiles or groups. To better search the network, users can use predefined categories and create their own categories. Categories can be used to sort profiles and groups of all directories. For example, if a user wants all profiles and groups of a certain economic sector, then the pie pieces represent the different sectors.
A toggle option in the upper control panel allows the user to switch whether all profiles and groups of a category are to be displayed or only the profiles with which the user has contact. A + next to the toggle button can be used to add second- and

third-degree contacts to the display. The user can extend the search to networked contacts, joined groups, followed groups and content that the user has marked as "interesting".

This function should make it possible for users to quickly build up a network with suitable participants in order to start any business. Using the search function, all networks can be searched for certain keywords, such as name, school class, professional skills or personal interests. If the search results are insufficient, the user can send a message to the entire network with his or her request.

12 Directories[52]

The directories facilitate cooperation between ministries and citizens. Citizens should be able to find contact persons quickly and reliably in order to implement political, entrepreneurial or private projects. Each ministry has a profile page in the State Directory, which also serves as its intranet page. Wherever state agencies regularly involve citizens and collect data about them, this information is stored in the directories and administered in cooperation between state employees and citizens. This allows citizens, on the one hand, to receive information about the work of ministries and, on the other hand, to view, add to, and check the accuracy and lawful retrieval of data collected about them, as well as to limit visibility to certain groups of persons. Limiting visibility for state employees who are legally entitled to do so is not possible.

All directories consist of profiles and groups through which multimedia content is made accessible in posts, comments, responses and ratings. The directories all use the same software and accordingly look the same from the user interface. Only their background colour is adapted to the colour of the ministry.

52§188,8,9 Statistics

12.1 Data shift between profiles

A special feature is the Persons Directory, where every citizen has a profile. What is special about these profiles is that all personal data is imported there from other directories and personal data is exported.

For example, a citizen has a profile in the Persons Directory, Education Directory and Labour Directory. His profile in the Education Directory is the profile of a learner who has attended courses and obtained degrees. To create the learner's profile, the learner's personal data, such as name, profile picture, age and place of residence, are exported from the profile in the Persons Directory to the profile in the Education Directory. Teachers keep a school record of the learner in their Education Directory profile. As soon as the learner graduates and leaves the educational institution, all data is transferred from the learner's profile in the Education Directory to the profile in the Persons Directory, i.e. imported. The profile in the Education Directory is deleted. If the citizen visits an educational institution again at a later time, all previously imported data is exported again to create a new profile in the Education Directory. If the citizen wishes to apply to a company as an employee, he or she creates a profile in the Labour Directory. All necessary data, from contact details to educational qualifications and testimonials, are taken from the profile in the Persons Directory, i.e. exported. If the citizen is still attending an educational institution, the data of the Education Directory profile can also be exported. With this data, an application can be automatically created in the Labour Directory profile. If the citizen then works in a company, the personnel file is kept in his or her profile in the Labour Directory. If the citizen opens a company, he creates a new profile in the Labour Directory and takes over all the necessary data from his profile as a worker and from his profile in the Persons Directory. If the citizen closes the company, all data is transferred to his profile in the Persons Directory and the profile of the company in the Labour Directory is deleted. If the citizen retires, all data from his profile as a worker in the Labour Directory are transferred to his profile in the Persons Directory and the worker's profile is deleted.

12.2 Profiles

Profiles represent someone or something. They are created by an authorised person and write rights are given to different authorised persons. Read rights are always given to the person creating the profile and to state employees who are legally authorised to do so.

For example, a citizen creates a profile in the Education Directory. The Residents' Registration Office has the right to write the imported personal data from the Persons Directory, such as name, date of birth and place of residence. The citizen cannot change this data, although he is the owner of this data and the profile in the Persons Directory. He has write access to his timetable, which no one else can change. Only the responsible teacher has write access to his or her school file.

The crucial point is that the citizen is the owner of all this data, because it was collected about him because of him. He can grant or deny reading rights to other persons. Every retrieval of data is considered a right to read.

Each profile has a pinboard on which viewers can leave posts, comments, replies or ratings. Profile creators can open additional noticeboards for specific topics.

12.3 Groups

Groups can either exist in a directory from the beginning or be created by users. Groups that are already there at the beginning cannot be closed, but groups created by users can.

In some directories, the profiles form the groups, such as in the Education Directory. There, the profiles of learners, teachers and researchers form a group for the educational institution they attend. In the Family Directory, although each youth centre has a profile, users can create a peer group in which their profiles from the Persons Directory are members. The peer group is not linked to the youth centre because peers can choose to visit the youth centre with their group or build a hut, for example.

Each group can determine which group of persons it is open to, or whether anyone can become a member and be able to post, comment or reply themselves. The first setting is made by the person who creates the group. Open groups can be joined by all users immediately. Closed groups, all users can send a request to join or they receive an invitation. Membership requests and invitations are answered or sent by the group leader. Users can leave groups at any time and thus terminate their membership. They can decide whether all or certain content they had ever created should remain in the group or be deleted.

Groups have at least one pinboard and any number of pinboards for topics that the group leaders can open. Group leaders are the users who have created a group. The group can re-elect group leaders via a deselection quorum of 75% of the group members. The group leader can distribute various administrative tasks to other group leaders. These group leaders also receive a deselection quorum. This quorum is not kept in the Quorum Directory, but is accessible on the group's homepage. Group members are entitled to vote. Group leaders or the system administrators of the digital service can close a group. Group leaders can only close a group if either there are no members left in the group or if they make this decision in voting with the group.

Groups can only be created by persons who are then personally responsible for the content. They are jointly responsible for offensive content that users repeatedly post. Group leaders can exclude members from the group. Group leaders who make decisions in voting with the group transfer joint responsibility to all members. Only the users who produce unlawful content or execute criminal offences are always responsible under criminal law.

12.4 Ratings

Users can rate posts, comments and answers and fill in surveys, both of which count as ratings. Contributions can be designed as polls and provide users with various answer options. This should make it possible to use all political processes, such as elections of persons, quorums, decision-making procedures in committees and voting, in a self-determined way on the intranet. To avoid confusion, voting by users on matters in the intranet is called "ratings". Votes are decisions made by those entitled to vote by citizens in the voting booths for the purpose of governance.[53]

12.5 Application Programming Interface for all directories

The Application Programming Interface is intended to enable users to automatically process data from the directories and use it for their own applications, for example games, news or statistics. All users can learn how to programme an Application Programming Interface in the Knowledge Directory. With the Application Programming Interface, they can flexibly create their own applications and make them available to all users at the same time. All programmed Application Programming Interface are entered in the Feedback Directory as a response in a profile for a new use case of directories. This allows users to check whether such an interface has already been made or whether there is an Application Programming Interface they can extend before programming their own new Application Programming Interface. All users who cannot or do not want to program an Application Programming Interface submit a request to the Ministry of Digital Affairs via the Feedback Directory to have such an Application Programming Interface programmed. The Ministry of Digital Affairs can then provide this Application Programming Interface as an answer in the request if it is useful for many users or if many users are in favour of it.

12.6 Homepage

The user can define the home page view himself by arranging, showing or hiding all the elements listed below as desired.

---

53   Ministry of State Organisation - 9.7 Voting

Left column	Centre	Right column
	Directory name	
Profile page	Last visitors to the page	Search bar and tab with scrollable list for categories
News service	-> Postal message	Search for institutions
Security settings	-> Video messages	Search for superiors
Own photos	-> Greetings	Search for persons
Own videos	-> Group invitations	Search for groups
Friends from the Persons Directory	-> Networking requests	Search for help
Network contact persons	-> Group messages	Administrator news
Network contact superiors	-> Invitations to meetings	Daily news
Network contact institutions	-> Contact request from an institution	Number of members of this directory
Own groups	Page visits from institutions	Total number of users now online Directory user count now online

12.7 Profile view

The profile view differs in whether it is a person or a thing. For example, persons have networks and reference persons, things have textures, opening hours or customers. Pinboards can be folded out via the + and folded in again via a -.

Directory name	Profile name	
Profile picture	Public data	
Texts	Location	
Images	+ Pinboard with fixed contributions	
Sounds	+ Pinboard with own contributions	
Videos	+ Pinboard with other person's contributions	

12.8 Post, comment and reply

Posts are made on noticeboards. Users can react to posts by commenting. Users can react to comments by replying to them. All three types of entries can be rated by other users via a participation bar. Authors can edit their entries at any time. The most recent edit is displayed. All edits are saved in the history of the entry, which can be viewed by users.

The directories go back to the Futaba software in terms of their programming, with which image boards can be created. The pinboards are the threads, topic-related pinboards are boards, contributions are posts. Users can write comments to posts and replies can be written to comments. Posts, comments and replies are called "entries" in the following for the sake of simplicity. Entries can be quoted by users, also known as hashtags.

<table>
<tr><td colspan="5">Directory</td><td colspan="5">Ministry</td></tr>
<tr><td colspan="10">Post, comment or reply: Title</td></tr>
<tr><td colspan="2">Image</td><td colspan="3">Name</td><td colspan="4">Keyword
Coordinate
System</td><td>Date</td></tr>
<tr><td colspan="10">Content of the news (text, sound, image, video)</td></tr>
<tr><td>+</td><td>-</td><td>I_</td><td>!</td><td>P</td><td>C</td><td>A</td><td><3</td><td>:D</td><td>:()</td><td>:(</td><td>:((</td></tr>
</table>

12.8.1 Sample process

12.8.1.1 Post

Legislative Directory		Ministry of State Organisation
Image	Keyword Coordinate System	Date
  Name: Andreas Seidl	 | Keywords:	Ministries:
---	---
Freedom	State organisation, Barter Economy, Planned Economy, Social Market Economy, Free Market Economy
Security	Security, Justice | Keywords that were relevant to create the point	03.03.2017 + = 56 564 523 - = 2 236 260 ! = 312 184

Content in the form of text, image, sound, video

Example content:
There should be four economic forms separated by "different currencies"(1) but existing in one country. Free and rich one is in the global market economy, Safe and rich one is in the national market economy, Safe and poor one is in the municipal economy, Free and poor one is in the natural economy. (2) The state thus offers the citizen "different levels of freedom and security"(3) , which in turn have different restrictions of place.

1in.labour.dir/profile-page-Ministry-of-Finance/currencies
2in.state.dir/Free Market Economy/We about us
 in.state.dir/Social Market Economy/About Us
 in.state.dir/Planned Economy/We about us
 in.state.dir/Barter Economy/We about us
3in.legisaltive.dir/group(Forms of economy)/Post(Resolve the dilemma of freedom vs. security!)/Comment(14.02.2017 22:36:01:56)

+	-		I_	!	P	C	A	<3	:D	:()	:(	:((

12.8.1.2 Comment

Image	Keyword Coordinate System	Date
Name: Max Mustermann	Freedom / Security (Pro / Contra)	15.03.2017 + = 26 258 140 - = 47 682 511 ! = 1 586

Keywords:	Ministries:
Freedom	State organisation, Barter Economy, Planned Economy, Social Market Economy, Foreign Affairs
Security	Security, Justice

I would abolish the Free Market Economy altogether and channel all foreign trade through the Ministry of Foreign Affairs.

+	-	I_	!	P	C	A	<3	:D	:()	:(	:((

12.8.1.3 Answer

Image	Keyword Coordinate System	Date
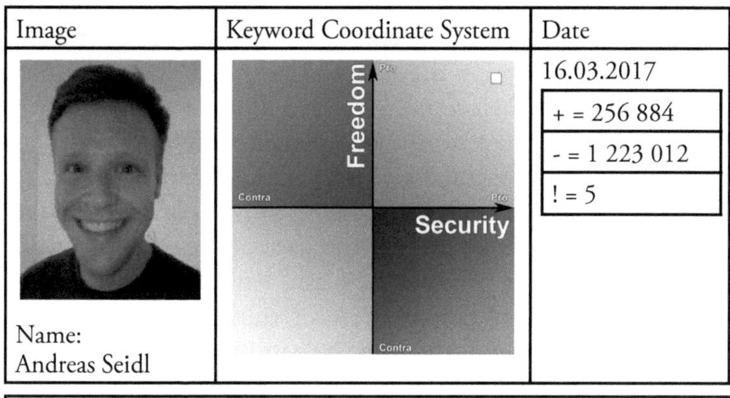 Name: Andreas Seidl		16.03.2017
		+ = 256 884
		- = 1 223 012
		! = 5

Then we would have planned economy, because the Ministry of Foreign Affairs was always responsible for foreign trade. But I would rather leave that in the hands of the entrepreneurs.	

+	-	I_	!	P	C	A	<3	:D	:()	:(	:((

12.8.2 Participation bar

This bar can be found under every post, every comment on a post and under every reply to a comment. As soon as a post, comment or reply is created via this bar, the reference of the new publication to the old publication that inspired the author to create it is displayed in the modulator.

+	-	I_	!	P	C	A
For this	Against this	Keyword Coordinate System	Mark & Cite	Create post	Create comment	Create answer

<3	:D	:()	:(	:((
In love	Amused	Amazed	Sad	Angry

The descriptions below are only displayed if you move the mouse pointer or finger over the symbol.

If the user presses For or Against, he or she indicates his or her attitude towards the entry.

If the user presses Keyword Coordinate System, he or she is shown which keywords the author of the entry has assigned and where the author of the entry locates his or her content. If the user shares this view, they can add the Keyword Coordinate System setting to their repository. This allows users to build up their own Keyword Coordinate System, which gets another pixel in a user's personal opinion picture with each entry. The user can view his or her opinion picture via the overview function. If votes are pending, the user can release his or her opinion picture for the Algoracle and have a voting decision proposed to him or her. If the user thinks that the author has given incorrect information, he can move the item in the Keyword Coordinate System. The programme collects this data, learns from it and transmits it to the author.

If you press Mark & Quote, the entire entry is marked and saved in your own clipboard. Users are automatically asked whether they want to include only the entry or the entire history of the associated post. If users themselves mark passages in the text or a file and then press Mark & Cite, only the marked content is included. The contents saved in the repository can be used in the following ways via the modulator. All stored content can be viewed in the overview function. Each entry can be quickly found and newly retrieved. As a filing aid in one's own repository, the information in the Keyword Coordinate System of the entry can be used to relate the entry to one's own opinion. The „Linker for sources" in the modulator can be used to specify the entry as a source when writing a new entry. This makes it possible for users to refer to or quote other users' contributions, comments and answers.

If the user presses post, comment or reply, the following entry is automatically linked to the entry under which the participation bar is placed.

If a user clicks on Amused, Amazed, Sad or Angry, he or she can express which feelings the entry has triggered in him or her.

12.9 Directory Register

Ministry	Directory	Profiles	Groups
Ministry of Labour	Labour Directory	Workforce, company	Company sports, associations, works councils, trade unions
	Success Model Directory	Success strategies	Model group
	Consumer Directory	Products	Consumer, supplier
	Food Directory	Food producers	Food
Ministry of Foreign Affairs	Travel Directory	Entry & Departure	Travel groups
Ministry of Education	Education Directory	Learners, Teachers, Researchers, Examinations Office, Education Authority	Educational institutions, project groups, research groups
	Knowledge Directory	Educational content	Fields of study, educational qualifications, research communities
Ministry of Family Affairs	Family Directory	Families, family assistance institutions	Peer reference groups
	Club Directory	Clubs, organisations	Joint offers and projects
Ministry of Finance	Tax Directory	Taxpayer	Tax brackets
Ministry of Health	Health Directory	Treating persons	Fields of study
	Care Directory	Care	Persons in need of care
	Environment Directory	Environmental damage	Disposal groups
Ministry of infrastructure	Infrastructure Directory	Building project	Assemblies, material database

	Real Estate Directory	Buildings, structures	Building opponents, owners, landlords, tenants
	Transport Directory	Transport links	Transport companies, carpools
	Energy Directory	Energy provider	Energy networks
Ministry of innovation	Ideas Directory	Inventions	Product group, inventor groups
	Research Directory	Research projects	Research groups
Ministry of Integration	Asylum Directory	Asylum seekers, refugees	Asylum Villages, Host Families
	Integration Directory	Foreigners, domestic citizens, guests, naturalised persons	Integration groups
Ministry of Digital Affairs	Access Directory	Data carrier	Groups of persons, examination groups
	Feedback Directory	People's Innovation Company Intranet Hardware & Software	Modder
Ministry of Justice	Law Directory	Norms	Codes of law, ministries, companies, clubs
	Court Directory	Cases	Courts
Ministry of Media Affairs	Media Directory	broadcasts	Broadcaster
	Format Directory	TV formats	Broadcasters and media
Ministry of Security	Investigation Directory	Cases	Closed investigator groups Open search groups
	Security Directory	security agencies	Services

Ministry of State organisation	Persons Directory	Citizens	Interest groups, circles of friends
	State Directory	Ministries	Departments, agencies
	Petition Directory	Petitions	Proponents, opponents
	Legislative Directory	Problems, norm proposals	Working groups of the parties, lobbyists
	Committee Directory	Committees	Visitor groups
	Quorum Directory	Quorums	Proponents, opponents
	Lobby Directory	Lobbyists Lobby representations	Companies, NGOs, advocates, opponents
Ministry of Barter Economy	Barter Economy Directory	Inhabitants	Settlements
Ministry of Planned Economy	Social Directory	Social Villages, Social Villagers	Work and leisure communities
Ministry of Social Market Economy	Farmer Directory	Farms	Cooperatives
Ministry of Free Market Economy			

13 People's Innovation Company Intranet[54]

The People's Innovation Company Intranet is a People's Innovation Company run by the Ministry of Digital Affairs. It constantly produces innovations to support the people with the latest Information Technology. It cannot be privatised because it is part of the fourth democratic power, the mediative.

The People's Innovation Company Intranet is responsible for the development of digital technologies used by the state. Its networks, devices, operating systems and programmes promote digitalisation and innovation. The People's Innovation

54§35,3 Political rights: BV Art.34, §207,2,5 Telecommunications: BV Art. 92, §113,8 Media democracy

Company Intranet provides the entire telematics structure, consisting of networks and devices for telecommunications as well as operating systems and programmes for information technology. The networks are developed and maintained in cooperation with the Ministry of Infrastructure.[55]

The People's Innovation Company Intranet, in voting with the ministries of state organisation and media, provides the hardware, software and digital services necessary for citizens to exercise their political rights. It equips citizens with transmitting and receiving devices to use the intranet at a cost-covering price. The production of goods takes place in secured buildings in the capital city of the Ministry of Digital Affairs and in Planned Enterprises[56] . Providers and co-producers are grouped together in an industrial community[57] . In voting with the Ministry of Foreign Affairs, common standards are agreed between the member states in a continental digital policy.

13.1 Production

The People's Innovation Company Intranet provides goods and services that can only be ordered, repaired and disposed of at the Intranet Café. Resale is prohibited. The devices are assembled in secured factories in the capital city of the Ministry of Digital Affairs.

The individual parts are produced in an industrial community consisting of domestic companies that are capable of fulfilling the orders. It does not play a role which economic form these companies belong to. All they have to do is fulfil the requirements and prove to be loyal secret keepers. The requirements include using only nationals to perform the tasks and employing them in accordance with the requirements of the Social Market Economy. All tasks that can also be carried out by Planned Enterprises must be performed there. Providers may only be domestic companies that produce the supplied goods inland and are specifically and increasingly monitored

---

55 Ministry of Infrastructure - 6.2.3 Data Network, 7 Digital Infrastructure
56 Ministry of Planned Economy - 10.5 Planned Enterprise
57 Ministry of Innovation - 10.4.1 Industrial communities

by the Company Auditing Agency.

The People's Innovation Company Intranet strives to recruit all staff from graduates of state educational institutions and, if possible, to retain them until retirement. Lateral entrants are only admitted in the absence of qualified graduates. All employees are sworn to secrecy, data protection and loyalty to the domestic people. The aim is to have as young and loyal staff as possible who are not willing to carry out or allow digital manipulation.

To prevent tampering, all devices that can be connected to the intranet are produced, sold, serviced and disposed of by the VIB intranet. People's Computers, accessories, transmission towers and servers are built in secured factories. The workplaces are under video surveillance.

The People's Innovation Company Intranet has several production sites, mainly in Social Villages, because they are fenced and there are voluntary workers who can also study computer science or electrical engineering part-time at the local college in this Social Village.

13.2 Hardware

The hardware includes all devices and lines that are necessary to operate the intranet. This mainly includes the People's Computer and its accessories, but also all computers used by state agencies to access the intranet. This includes the computers in the ministries and the intranet cafés, as well as the voting computers in the polling booths. All data that is not stored on the People's Computers is stored by the Ministry of Digital Affairs in its own secured servers that are distributed in a decentralised manner. Backup copies are stored once a day on the high-security servers of the Ministry of Digital Affairs. All hardware is designed in such a way that the intranet is secured and operated autonomously from the Internet and other foreign terminal devices. People's Computers are connected via radio signals to transmission towers, which send the signal through their own intranet lines within the country and access the servers of the Ministry of Digital Affairs in order to network. The same applies to computers in the ministries and polling booths, but they are connected directly to the intranet line and not through a radio signal.

13.3 Software

The People's Innovation Company Intranet produces software, namely programmes and operating systems used on the networks' switchboards, servers, computers and People's Computers. The source code of all software is open. By disclosing the source code, everyone can participate in the search for security vulnerabilities. Already existing open source software, such as the operating system Linux[58] , the browser Firefox[59] or the EDP programme LibreOffice[60] , is included in the creation of programmes for the intranet. Only software that has been tested for a long time and functions stably is used. This is to avoid the occurrence of security gaps that could be used by hackers for attacks. As soon as security gaps are found, security updates are carried out as quickly as possible.

Users can download all programmes, updates and modifications free of charge from the intranet site of the Ministry of Digital Affairs in the State Directory. A link to the Feedback Directory can also be found there, through which all programmes and modifications there are included in the media library of programmes. In some cases it is only possible to download parts of programmes because these programmes require more computing power than the People's Computer has. These programmes are managed via the intranet by the user sending commands and data via his People's Computer to the server of the Ministry of Digital Affairs, where the programme is executed. Memory states and finished files can be transferred to the People's Computer.

58https://www.linux.org/pages/download/
59https://www.mozilla.org/de/firefox/new/
60https://de.libreoffice.org/

13.3.1 Software development

Ministries and citizens can request programmes or intranet pages with various functions. Every wish is published in the Feedback Directory, unless the Security or Ministry of Justice orders secrecy. Users can rate the wishes for new software in the Feedback Directory. If 50% of the users agree, a test version is made available, which all users are then asked to rate. The test ends after 30 days. If 75% of the users decide in favour of the new version, it will be introduced.

Ministers can commission programmes on their own, without waiting for a user vote. Ministries must solicit the costs for these programmes or functions in the budget vote.

Software development is carried out firstly by programmers from the Ministry of Digital Affairs, secondly by graduates from educational institutions and thirdly by voluntary users (modders). The programmers are employees of the People's Innovation Company Intranet and work in the capital city of the Ministry of Digital Affairs or Social Villages in secured areas. Graduates of educational institutions can complete their own programme, a programme from the wish list or a specific commissioned work in the subject of computer science as their final thesis. By dividing the work among all the graduates of all the educational institutions, all the examinees can write part of a programme and the entire graduating class works together to produce the desired programme. Voluntary users are persons who know how to programme and write programmes or modifications (mods) for programmes in their spare time and collaborate via the Feedback Directory.

At state colleges, prize competitions are held for computer science students. There is prize money for the best programme and a job offer on the People's Innovation Company intranet.

13.3.2 Update

All updates are created by programmers from the Ministry of Digital Affairs and voluntary users. Users can submit their proposals to the Ministry of Digital Affairs via the Feedback Directory. All newly programmed proposals, whether from users or programmers, are displayed on the homepage for all users. All users now have the possibility to use the new version as a test version and to switch it off again.

So once the entire operating system is completely revised in terms of its usability, there must have been many popular innovations. However, there are memory levels that each user can set personally. Once a user has familiarised himself with the system and its programme structure, he usually becomes slower in using it because, firstly, he is not so familiar with its use and, secondly, he misses old ways of operating it. Therefore, every user can save his or her current user interface in the way that best suits him or her. All updates that have to do with the user interface fall under the category of saveable operating system settings.

For data security reasons, the source code of the operating system must be renewed every year. Every year, the source code of the operating system is completely renewed via an update. Every year, the users are asked whether they would like to change the operation or the appearance of the operating system, and if so, which change. Every year, one month after the budget vote, all popular proposals are offered to the users as beta versions for use. This way, all new features can be tested and rated individually. As soon as a feature achieves the quorum of 75% of users, the innovation is introduced after the next update. In addition to the beta versions, the last 10 versions of the operating system are always available, as well as one's own configurations that one has deselected or selected in the course of the innovations. One can save the operating version of one's People's Computer.

Another option is the overview of all versions of all operating systems. Here, users can wish back for old features. Each version has a superscript that shows how many endorsements there are for that version in total. If you click on the high number, you will see a list of all the most popular features of a version.

13.4 Feedback Directory

In the Feedback Directory, users can make their proposals on the design, content, function of directories, intranet pages, programmes or data security and download any software with open source code free of charge. In this directory, all directories, intranet pages, programmes or data security measures have a profile. Users can publish technical faults (bugs) or suggestions for improvements (mods). Users can form groups to jointly programme improvements, So-called modder groups, which can each specialise in one software of the People's Innovation Company Intranet. Faults are fixed and suggestions for improvements are displayed to all users on the start page so that they can be voted on according to popularity and introduced if they are sufficiently popular.
Each Directory links its "Help Page" to its profile in the Feedback Directory. All existing Application Programming Interfaces can be accessed via the Feedback Directory and can also be used for other directories.

13.5 Financing

The People's Innovation Company Intranet finances its services from tax revenue, fees and sales prices. All pages and programmes of the intranet that are used for state management, as well as the equipment and use of the intranet café, is Tax-funded. The first People's Computer, given as a 10th birthday present, is also Tax-funded.
All devices, except the first People's Computer, advertisements and certain programmes and simulations are subject to a charge. For People's Computers, the cost-covering price applies. For all other devices, 10% is added to the cost-covering price as profits. Fees are charged for advertisements and certain programmes and simulations. Programmes subject to fees include digital company management and market simulation for Free Market Economy companies.
The intranet in itself generates economic growth and thus increasing tax revenues because nationals, as owners of a company, are allowed to use the intranet for their economic

activities, regardless of what economic form they come from. The intranet represents a natural monopoly. The initial investment is high, but supporting another unit is vanishingly small in comparison. The fact that the cables only have to be laid once and the last metres to the end user are covered wirelessly means that this is a one-off investment, as are the new companies that have to be set up for the devices and the operating system. Once the system is up and running, it generates content through its users that serves the state for its population statistics, law enforcement, election and legislative processes. In this way, the state saves costs that were previously produced on an ongoing basis, such as postal and ballot elections, censuses, registration and postal correspondence.

13.5.1 Costs for the People's Computer

Only the first People's Computer is given to a citizen on his or her tenth birthday. If it becomes unusable due to damage or is lost, the replacement device must be paid for. The costs amount to the current production costs and delivery charges. However, if a new model appears because technical development is advancing, the new device must be purchased on a hire-purchase basis over a period of 5 years. However, this obligation to purchase to participate in direct democracy may only affect a citizen a maximum of three times in his or her lifetime. If it happens more often, the state must bear these costs.

13.5.2 Advertising

Companies from the four economic forms can place advertisements on the intranet under different conditions. The digital service markets the advertising and allows the type and location of the advertising to be adapted to the appropriate target group.
Newly established Experimental Enterprises and Innovation

Enterprises[61] can advertise their goods and services they want to export to the market economy on the Intranet. They can pay the costs in instalments, which only have to be paid if profits are made and do not exceed 20% of the profits.

Social Market Economy companies can place advertisements and only have to pay the price as soon as they generate additional profits with them. An instalment payment is agreed, the monthly amounts of which are deducted from the additional profits generated by the advertising. Instalments of 20 to 100 per cent of the additional profits can be set by the companies as payments, which they settle monthly until the price of the advertising measures has been paid off. The measurements of the additional profits are verified by the Company Auditing Agency as part of its regular audits.

Domestic companies in the Barter Economy and Free Market Economy can place advertisements whose time slot has a fixed price. Discounts or payment by instalments are not possible.

13.5.3 Simulations for persons and companies

All persons and companies that feed all their data into the intranet pay less for simulations. The price per simulation, is measured by the prices given by other persons and companies whose data is to be included in the simulation. Companies can therefore specify in the Labour Directory how much money they charge for their data. Persons do this in the Persons Directory. An input field next to the personal data can be used to specify a price for simulations that are subject to a charge. The data can also be priced as a bundle. The Ministry of Digital Affairs charges a 10% surcharge for each price.

13.6 People's Computer

The People's Computer is the transmitting and receiving devices that enable citizens to make legal personal digital contact with each other and with the state. It serves as an

---

61 Ministry of Planned Economy - 10.8 Experimental Enterprises, 10.6 Innovation Enterprises

interface to allow the brains of the citizens to become a meta-brain of the state. The citizen thus becomes a cell in the body of the state, contributing to its function and management. This device empowers every citizen to participate in the policy-making of the inland. In addition, the People's Computer offers all the advantages of social networks known from the Internet, but improves them significantly. The improvements are data security in every respect, because all users are registered with their identity card and will therefore behave lawfully, because law enforcement is so easy. So those who value legality and reliability can use the intranet free of charge. The use of the People's Computer and Intranet access is not possible abroad. The People's Innovation Company Intranet is responsible for building the People's Computer, including hardware and software. The People's Computer is the mass product of the People's Innovation Company Intranet. There is a standard variant and any number of extended models. The standard version is given to every nationals on their tenth birthday as a permanent loan. Legally, the People's Computer remains the property of the people, just like any other identity card. All other models must be purchased. All devices come with a lifetime guarantee. The device is used to enable the domestic population to communicate and act in a tap-proof, fraud-free, constitutional and notarised environment. Trade in the devices takes place in the town hall's intranet café. Repair orders are also accepted here.

13.6.1 Operating system

The operating system for the People's Computer is similar to Linux. It offers the user access to programmes and devices such as a camera or microphone that are built into the People's Computer. This can be used to work offline. A word processing programme is pre-installed for writing texts, screenplays, presentations or tables. The browser for the intranet is the People's Navigator, which is also pre-installed and automatically connects to the intranet.

13.6.2 First activation

The first login to the People's Computer or computer of an Intranet Café, must be received by a staff member of the Ministry of Digital Affairs in the Intranet Café of the Town Hall. It proceeds in three steps. First, one has to think of a four-digit number combination and enter it covertly into an input device with a dial. This becomes the personal PIN number. Second, you have to hold your guide eye in front of the iris scanner. The guide eye is determined by a test. This is done by standing one metre away from the screen. A small red dot appears in the middle of the white screen. You now have to look at the dot with both eyes while bringing both hands together in a circle in front of your face so that the dot is circled by your hands. Now close the left eye and then the right eye alternately. The eye that is looking at the dot is the leading eye. Thirdly, you have to sign your name on a touchpad in the intranet café in front of the eyes of a staff member who then compares the signature with the signature on the back of the identity card.

The Ministry of Digital Affairs worker works in the intranet café and has a special ID card reader and writer. This can be used to match the PIN code, iris, signature and fingerprint data with the data in the identity card. From then on, the identity card is used to be recognised by a People's Computer or computer in the intranet café and to match the data in the expulsion card with the characteristics of the person before it is used.

13.6.3 Use

People's Computers can be used to surf the intranet, use programmes and directories, navigate and make phone calls with or without a picture. People's Computers are personal and cannot be lent out, given or sold to another user. Anyone who wants to give accessories or a second device as a gift must buy a voucher for it in the Intranet Café. Anyone who does not want to use the People's Computer must return it to the Intranet Café. There are always replacement devices and loaners available there in their current condition. All transactions that can be made via the People's Computer can also be made with the computers in the Intranet Café.

13.6.4 Residence

Nationals do not have to have a permanent residence because all the state's data is transmitted to them on the People's Computer. People's Computers should always be kept at home if possible. Should a visit be necessary, the People's Computer is used to request whether the address of the nationals may be determined with a location query. Only the police are allowed to query the locations secretly until the court proceedings are over or the case is finally closed. After that, the data query must be entered in the Access Directory, which the owner of the People's Computer can view at any time. If you move and the People's Computer stays in another place for more than three months, you will automatically be asked if you have moved. If you want to report your move immediately, click on "Retrieve new residence" in the Persons Directory.

13.6.5 Liability

People's Computer users are personally liable for any offences they commit with the device. People's Computers are not allowed to leave the domestic territory. Anyone who crosses the border with the People's Computer will be punished. A sensor registers attempts to open the device and border crossings. In both cases, the People's Computer sends a final signal to the Ministry of Digital Affairs with its location and the last identity card registered, which is usually always the same. After that, the data storage in the People's Computer automatically self-destructs. The nationals are immediately put on the wanted list and brought before a judge at the next possible opportunity. After an examination of the device and the facts, a decision is made whether to impose a fine of 1000 Dollars plus the cost of the new replacement device or imprisonment for a maximum of 10 years.

Lost People's Computers are located and recovered by the

police. Provided that all individual parts can be recovered and espionage activity can be ruled out, the owner gets off scot-free and only has to pay for the new device.

Voting computers must not leave the Intranet Café or they will destroy themselves. Unused People's Computers must be brought to the Intranet Café and locked up for decommissioning.

The People's Innovation Company Intranet develops the exact security concept, especially when the destruction of the hard disk with the encrypted data of the private person is necessary. Data security should be guaranteed. Any attempts to manipulate the People's Computer must be able to be detected immediately. The integrity of the software is checked by checksums (hash value) .[62]

13.6.6 Locating

If a People's Computer is lost, the owner of the People's Computer must report it to the police immediately. First of all, the People's Computer's position is located by satellite and radio network. If the owner knows the location, he can retrieve the People's Computer himself and report it via the People's Computer. To do this, go to the Access Directory and search for the most recent accesses, which originate from the radio and satellite location by the police. There, the owner now clicks on the checkmark "found".

If the location indicated by the tracking is not known to the owner and a data theft could be possible, the police destroy the data carriers of the People's Computer. The command to destroy the People's Computer's hard disk and memory is issued remotely. The same command is automatically received when a People's Computer moves out of the country. For this purpose, each hard disk carries an integrated explosive device. However, the hard drive and RAM are encased in a secure shell so that the explosion will only dent the shell and not injure any persons. Through the integrated battery, the People's Computer continues to transmit its position to the police. The police tell the owner the position and he

62https://de.wikipedia.org/wiki/Hashfunktion

can decide whether to repeat his People's Computer with or without police protection. The People's Computer looks the same from the outside after the internal destruction. After the destruction, one receives a receipt from the police, with which one can buy a new People's Computer in the intranet café. Destroyed or defective People's Computers can be exchanged for a new People's Computer at any intranet café in the local town hall for a repair fee for the old unit.

13.6.7 Audit

Every People's Computer is audited by the Company Auditing Agency every 3 years and is awarded a badge for a successful audit. Technical auditors from the Company Auditing Agency[63] regularly visit the intranet cafés and announce their appointments a year in advance. They set up testing racks. Citizens have to switch on their People's Computer and go onto the intranet. Then the auditor places the People's Computer in a compartment on the shelf. Wirelessly, the shelf connects to the People's Computer and reads the data for tampering attempts and faults. If a People's Computer is defective, the data is immediately backed up there and transferred to a replacement device, which the citizen can then take and keep. The old device is repaired and issued to a citizen again.
The service fee at the examination finances the maintenance and updating of software and hardware.

13.6.8 Standard model

The People's Computer is an A4-sized tablet PC without external connectivity. Power is supplied by induction charging of two rechargeable batteries. One battery is necessary for operation. The other battery is used to store the device even when the battery is empty without losing data. Charging is done via a plug that has a magnetic induction surface that can be attached to the given magnetic spot on the People's Computer.

63Ministry of Labour - 20.7.4 Technical auditor

The device is operated via a touch screen that covers the entire front. There are two loudspeakers on the back, a 3D camera with sliding cover and a 2D camera on the front with sliding cover. A microphone is embedded in a kind of ear canal on the underside, which can be closed with a plug. The plug and sliding cover are manual functions to automatically exclude unauthorised surveillance. On the top there is a slot for the identity card. As soon as the identity card is expelled, the People's Computer switches on. As soon as it is pulled out, the People's Computer switches off again. Registration is done by scanning the iris, facial recognition, PIN number and fingerprint. This security also allows company secrets and ideas for inventions to be shared with a freely selectable number of users without fear of theft or manipulation of data. The device is waterproof up to a depth of 2 metres.

13.6.9 Extensions[64]

Headphones, hands-free devices, keyboards, mice, tripods, bags, GPS bracelets and much more are constantly being redesigned by the creative staff of the People's Innovation Company Intranet. Citizens' wishes are catered for. Other models of the People's Computer can be larger or smaller, have integrated retractable 360° 3D cameras, small projectors with a touch-active projection surface, Virtual Reality glasses or similar variations. By manufacturing all components and models in-house, crimes such as data theft, computer viruses or malicious software can be avoided via the intranet.

Many extensions are suitable for carrying out digital training in the Knowledge Directory. The characteristics of these extensions are defined by the ministries for digital affairs, education, security, media, innovation, work and the economy together with the People's Innovation Company Intranet. The aim is to make digital training as close as possible to professional activities and teaching.

Other devices for official use by the ministries are produced on their orders and delivered to them. The Ministry of Security will receive a variant that fits in a trouser pocket and can be

---

64 §182.1 Further education: BV Art. 64a

used as a walkie-talkie.[65]

13.6.9.1 Virtual reality glasses

The Virtual Reality glasses are available in a transparent and an opaque version. One version is closed, similar to the Virtual Reality glasses of the Playstation 4[66] and the other version is transparent, like the HoloLens from Microsoft[67]. The opaque version allows the People's Computer to be operated without being observed. It is used for oral exams, for example. The transparent version offers a reality enhanced by virtual components. These glasses have cameras that can recognise objects and environments. This version is used at work to record materials and work steps, as well as to digitally coordinate stock levels and assembly line work. Schools and training companies can use them to digitise operations and trainees can use the operations as a model while practising a work step. The glasses are able to capture all moving objects while the wearer stands still. To avoid costly greenbox shots, rooms, backgrounds and objects that are stationary can be removed. Moving objects can be removed by left winking or clicking. In this way, activities can be cut out and faded into reality on the transparent glasses.

13.6.9.2 Cash register

Companies must use a cash register for their economic activities involving cash. The cash registers are able to scan banknotes and weigh coins that are inserted into them. They automatically reconcile the amount of money in the cash register with the stored cash receipts and transmit the data via the intranet to the Ministry of Finance and to the company's profile in the Labour Directory.[68]

---

65 Ministry of Security - 4.2 Radio traffic
66 https://www.playstation.com/de-de/explore/playstation-vr/
67 https://www.microsoft.com/en-us/hololens
68 Ministry of Finance - 5.2.3 Cash, 11.6.2 Tax account for companies

14 Programmes[69]

Programmes are digital tools that enable users to administer, shape and predict their private, business and political relationships. To do this, the Ministry of Digital Affairs creates programmes that can collect, display, store and link data inputs from citizens and the state. The Ministry of Digital Affairs receives suggestions or orders from other ministries or users to expand existing programmes or create new ones.

14.1 Homepage

Users who want to open a programme select the start page for programmes in the operating system. All programmes are listed on the start page. Each user can place selected programmes on the start page as a linker that he or she has installed or uses online. The list is sorted either alphabetically, according to the last or longest use.

The start page also always displays the administrators' news. As soon as a programme is due for an update, this is announced on the start page. If the update is intended to change the use of certain contents, this version is made available as a user test by means of a link in the news message. After the user trial, users can vote on whether they prefer the new version or the current way of using it. Depending on which programmes a user uses, only these updates are displayed.

14.2 Answer Finder

The Answer Finder is the intranet's search engine that makes directories, intranet pages and databases searchable. It is structured similarly to Google's advanced search. In the middle is the long search bar, where keywords or questions can be entered. To get answers to questions, users can enter the questions as follows. Above the search bar are coloured blocks with the following words on them: Noun, Verb, Adjective, Article, Who, Where, How, What, Why. Each block can be moved into the search bar, even several times. The building

---

69 §207,4,6 Telecommunications

blocks article, noun, verb and adjective can be labelled with the appropriate words as soon as they are in the search bar. This is how you can enter your question. As soon as nouns, verbs, adjectives and articles already exist as keywords, they are proposed to the user as he enters them.

14.2.1 Narrow search

Under the search bar, the search requests can be narrowed down. The "Date" button can be used to limit the search from a date, to a date or from a date to another date. The "Radius" button can be used to enter a postcode or an address and a radius in metres to limit the search to this radius. The "Subject" button can be used to select subject areas to which the search is to be limited. The subject areas can be entered via an input bar, whereby linked keywords are already predefined during the input. If a subject area is not available, no linked keyword appears. Next to the input bar, you can use the "List" button to display all existing subject areas and tick individual ones to select them. Multiple entries are possible. The search can also be limited to certain ministries, directories or groups of directories. Using the "Ministry" button, one or more ministries can be ticked from a list of 18 to limit the search to them. The same applies to directories and groups. The search limits do not have to be used. You can also simply type in the question.

14.2.2 Display of the results

As soon as the input has been confirmed, the results appear. The results with the highest probability of being correct and the lowest error quotient are displayed at the top. The results can be displayed sorted by subject area, date, radius, frequency of calls, ministry, directory or group.
It is possible that a similar question has already been asked. In this case, the answers are displayed one below the other. Those marked as "checked" are displayed first, then those rated as "correct" and then all other answers that have not

been marked as "wrong" by questioners.

However, if there is not yet an answer to a question, the question will appear on the Answer Finder home page at the bottom of the screen and will be displayed in the news in the appropriate directories or appropriate groups dealing with that topic. Anyone who might know the answer should answer it.

14.2.3 Finding the right answers

All questions can be answered and rated by all users. If the questioner was able to determine the answer to be wrong through a test, he or she presses "wrong". The answer then disappears again. If a questioner presses "correct" because the answer has indeed helped him or she was able to test it as correct, this correct answer appears directly below the question and no longer in chronological order of entry below each other. If questions and correct answers match, they are added to the question catalogue and stored in the Knowledge Directory. The new entry in the Knowledge Directory automatically sends a check request to the responsible subject areas of the state educational institutions. They check the questions and answers and can also call in experts from state institutes[70] or the Company Auditing Agency for the examination. If there are faults in an answer, the auditor should improve it. Once the examination has been carried out, the answer is given a mark in the top right-hand corner with the words "examined". If the judgement is ambiguous, a percentage probability is given, for example "89% correct". A verdict is only inconclusive if science does not know any better to date.

14.3 Swap shop

The swap shop can be accessed via the Labour Directory and Barter Economy Directory. In this swap shop, all goods and services can be exchanged for goods, services or money, sorted by economic forms, industries and locations. Similar to ebay

---

70 Ministry of Education - 11.7.2 State research institutes

classifieds[71] , offers and requests from all over the country are listed there. Each exchange for money is charged with 1% profit mark-up for the Ministry of Barter Economy. The citizens and entrepreneurs of the Barter Economy can use this platform as a virtual marketplace to import and export goods or services more easily.

14.4 Open Leaks

Through this programme, whistleblowers who wish to remain anonymous can submit digital evidence of crimes. It is part of the fourth power, the mediative, to control other powers in the state.[72] Citizens can also report suspected crimes to the police at any time and hand over the evidence to the responsible investigators for prosecution. Evidence of alleged crimes by politicians or other state employees can also be handed over by citizens to Surveillance Television[73] , the External Service of the Federal Moderator's Office[74] and the Audit Court[75] to initiate a prosecution. Law enforcement authorities have a duty to review all Open Leaks publications and prosecute domestic cases.

Open Leaks is a database with artificial intelligence and profile pages including a noticeboard and data repository that are freely accessible. Open Leaks can be accessed via the internet and the intranet. On the internet, data is published in full as soon as it is uploaded by whistleblowers. The public is supposed to determine the authenticity and provide evidence for or against it on the publication noticeboard.

The data is only published on the intranet if it does not endanger any bystanders. The ministries of security and justice check the authenticity of the data and publish it afterwards, regardless of the result of the check. Uninvolved persons are made unrecognisable. If a sufficient number of citizens have doubts, they can force the publication of the unprocessed data by means of a veto quorum. Whistleblowers do not receive a

71https://www.ebay-kleinanzeigen.de/
72Ministry of State Organisation - 12.5.1 Open Leaks
73Ministry of Media - 12 Surveillance Television
74Ministry of State Organisation - 4.4.2 External Service
75Ministry of Finance - 9.7 Audit Court

sentence, but if necessary a witness protection programme.

The programme is designed to compare data from the database with all laws and to automatically display violations. In order to make the algorithm in the programme understand the course of the offence, the informant virtually represents the course of the offence. The input mask resembles a hearing form in which many keywords are requested in order to be able to establish the connection to the affected laws. Finally, the course of events is represented by a simulation on the virtual inland map in the People's Navigator. By looking at the simulation, the informant checks whether the algorithm has correctly understood the course of events.

As a result, the programme provides all responsible state employees sorted by ministry. Via a linker, the results of Open Leaks can be shared on the internet and intranet. The programme is similar to a dragnet for politicians and shows conspicuous actions. The aim is to be able to quickly check whether politicians have violated laws or broken election promises. In order to make the decision for a deselection quorum[76] , personal information about the user's opinion can also be compared with the professional behaviour of the politician.

14.5 Modulator

The Modulator is used to map the abundance of entries in the directories and their links with each other. It is an interface between all directories and gives users the possibility to administer all their read, rated and self-created entries.

Because a different view or mode of operation is required depending on the type of application, the modulator offers various modules that make different applications possible.

Each noticeboard on the intranet is a forum where users can discuss. The Modulator offers add-on modules that are an extension to the software of the directories. The People's Navigator can be used to install the Modulator as an additional companion application.

To make all entries in a digital network more easily visible

76Ministry of State Organisation - 9.5.10 Deselection quorum

and searchable, there is an overview function and a coordinate system of opposing keywords on the X and Y axes, the So-called Keyword Coordinate System.

14.5.1 Anonymiser

In order to be able to conduct discussions objectively, it can sometimes be helpful for all participants to discuss with each other anonymously. This is to be able to separate factual contributions from the author and to eliminate prejudices against the person of the author. This function can be applied in any policy discussion of the Comment Modulator by any user in the form of a newly created group. Similar to the proposal to hold a secret voting.

The anonymiser can be switched on for pinboards or posts. All subsequent entries will then be anonymised. Anonymisation can only be removed if all affected users agree. The anonymisation provides for two stages. In the first stage, all participants are automatically assigned consecutive numbers. Users can thus recognise which participant makes repeated comments. In the second stage, entries are only given time stamps. Those who comment repeatedly or for the first time cannot be identified.

14.5.2 Negotiator

This module helps to formulate texts for treaties or laws and to make many changes by many persons to the text possible and comprehensible. As soon as a text is marked and copied, it can be inserted and negotiated. The user interface is a screen split down the middle with two columns. On the left is the original text, and on the right are the deletions and changes made by other users, which can be rated. The original text is the contribution, so to speak, and the deletions and changes are the comments. There are no replies here, only the rating function allows users to respond with approval or disapproval.

14.5.3 Keyword Coordinate System

The Keyword Coordinate System is a multifaceted representation system for personal attitudes. Because politics is about more areas of tension than just "right or left", any keywords can be used here, each of which is linked to at least one ministry. Because each entry has a Keyword Coordinate System, it is clear in which ministry the competences lie and which party wing is represented by an opinion or formulation. In addition, users can assess content more quickly and search for it more specifically.

14.5.3.1 Creation of a Keyword Coordinate System

Authors of an entry must provide information about the location in the Keyword Coordinate System. Each author of an entry can select the keywords for the X- and Y-axis from a categorised selection list. In the selection list, the frequency with which the keyword was used is shown in brackets after the keyword. If a decider chooses a keyword from one axis, keywords that are most frequently used on the other axis are displayed in bold in the selection list. Again, the frequency number of the respective keyword is shown in brackets.
If a suitable keyword does not yet exist, it can be newly created. Newly created keywords must be assigned to at least one ministry and other categories, such as economic sectors.
Comments and replies always adopt the two predefined keywords of the post to which they refer. However, the authors of comments and replies can choose the election in the Keyword Coordinate System themselves. By pressing the button "Determine point automatically", an algorithm determines which keywords are present in the content of the entry and for which page they stand. This process is displayed for the user. All keywords in the content are marked in colour. The colour corresponds to the location in the Keyword Coordinate System. If the keywords are written in *italics*, they refer to the keyword of the X-axis. If the author detects an error in the algorithm, he can correct it. The programme behind the algorithm is thus constantly learning.

Example

A classic example of policy is the tension between freedom and security. Security would be on the X-axis and freedom on the Y-axis. If the discussion were about how one wants to live in the future, different statements would be evaluated as follows. "I want to be free as a bird and not abide by any laws." The point here would be in the negative far left area on the X-axis, and in the positive upper area on the Y-axis. (Light red) The opposite would be the case with the following statement. "I don't want anything to happen to me and I'm willing to live in prison for it." The point here would be in the positive far right area on the X-axis, and in the negative lower area on the Y-axis. (Light blue)

Security is a buzzword linked to the Ministry of Security and the Ministry of Justice. Freedom is a keyword linked to the Ministry of Family Affairs and the Ministries of Economy.

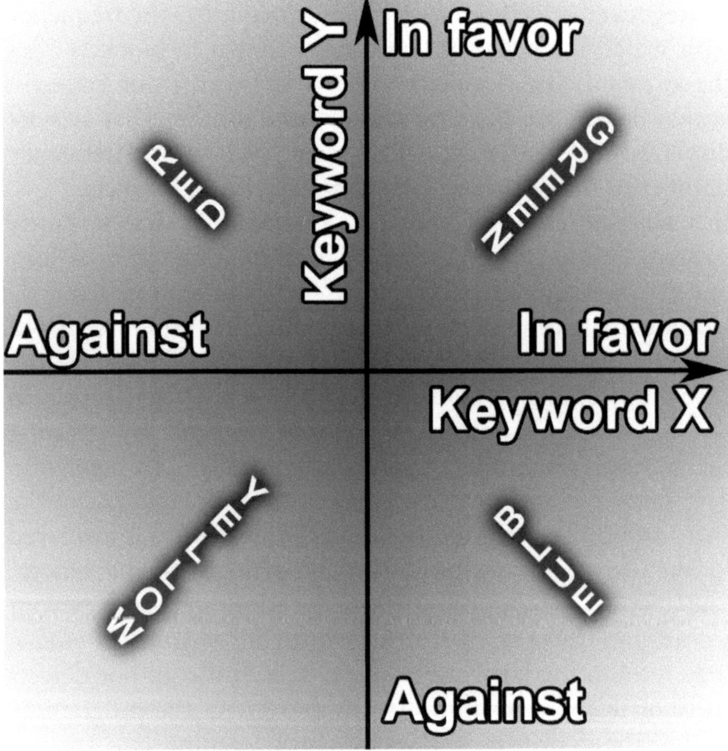

14.5.4 Overview function

The overview function offers the user various forms of display. To select a directory, there is the tree structure, the pie chart and the circle view. To view one's own entries and ratings clearly, there is the layer view and the personal Keyword Coordinate System.

The layer view is similar to a sociogram, showing how you reacted to someone or how someone reacted to you. The digital interactions with users and opinions become manageable and traceable so that you can administer your personal network.

14.5.4.1 Mindmap

The view can be imagined like a fir tree viewed from above. In the centre, the trunk, is the user. At the very top, there is a small level with a few branches and ramifications. Below that, there are other levels that get bigger and bigger with increasingly longer branches and ramifications. The branches symbolise the directories, profiles or groups where pinboards are. The branches symbolise the posts, with further branching to comments and replies. The trunk symbolises the user himself, to whose data the overview function refers.

The user can use the levels as categories, which he or she determines. The default setting is the chronological order of the entries. The most recent entries are at the top, and the entries for the past month, year and decade are at the levels below.

To narrow the view to less content, data can be entered for time periods, groups of persons, ministries, directories, profiles, groups or keywords. All posts, comments or replies that relate to the same topic are now displayed. A focus function allows users to move through the levels and branches from top to bottom.

The user can relate the entries to each other by creating further categories. For example, each directory from which entries originate can be a category, or positive ratings, emotions or comments that one has given. In the categorical view, the categories are the levels of the tree with their branches. The user can connect the chronological sequence to a category and see the bindings between the levels. In this display, the view pans from the two-dimensional bird's-eye view to the three-dimensional first-person perspective. Connecting lines between the branches of different levels show temporal developments in a category.

14.5.4.2 Personal opinion in the coordinate system

The personal opinion survey is structured like a Keyword Coordinate System, but it has a lot of points. The user can select any keyword on the X and Y axis. Each point stands for the point in the Keyword Coordinate System of an entry that the user has either read, quoted, created, commented on, answered, saved, rated emotionally, disapproved of or agreed with. The user can choose which of his or her activities to display. The programme searches for all keywords in the entries, even if only one of the two keywords is applicable in the Keyword Coordinate System of an entry. Points on the X or Y axis are entries without a matching second keyword in the Keyword Coordinate System of the entry. All points that do not lie on the axes come from entries where both keywords determined by the user were also selected by the author of the entries. Points that lie in the same place are stacked. Through this three-dimensional coordinate system, users can see how their own opinion is justified in relation to equal or opposite opinions. The reasons for this lie in the content of the entries. In the Algoracle, this data can be introduced by the user to provide decision-making aids for political or personal deciders of the user.

14.5.5 Linker for sources

Users can use the Linker while writing an entry. It serves the users to be able to substantiate their statements or contents in entries with sources. All digital sources from the internet and intranet are displayed as a retrievable link. Internet sources can be exported via a companion application for internet browsers. The data is exported via servers of the Ministry of Digital Affairs and sent to the user's linker on the intranet.

As a programme, the Linker is an extension of the People's Navigator search function. In the left-hand control panel is the familiar search function. In addition to the search functions of the People's Navigator, entries can also be searched for in the overview function of the modulator.

All search results can be viewed as usual. In the upper control panel for management, an additional button can be used to copy the source citation. If the user presses the button "Create source citation", the source is displayed in the bottom left-hand corner, which will later be inserted into his or her entry. If the user wants to quote or paraphrase foreign content, he or she can do so using the Linker. To paraphrase, the user inserts the source into his or her entry without having previously marked any content and generally refers to the source.

The user quotes certain content by marking it, copying it and pasting it into his or her entry. As soon as one has written one's entry, one can mark individual parts in it in which one refers to a foreign source. Users mark lines of text by holding down the mouse button and a rubber band frame or by selecting the section in the timeline of the video or audio recording by holding down the mouse button. As soon as the marks are highlighted in blue, "Create quote" can be clicked on in the upper control panel.

Each source citation contains a timestamp. If the source is not available digitally, its location is indicated. At the bottom left of the source, there is a button that allows you to link the source to your entry. Other users viewing the entry can see the source information as a footnote and follow digital links.

14.5.6 Connector with opinions

Users can use the Connector to find equal or opposite opinions compared to an entry. As soon as an entry is displayed or created in the middle panel, the Connector can be activated in the right panel.

At the top right, a slider is displayed with "compromise" at one end and "coalition" at the other. "Compromise" is used to

display entries that represent an opposing opinion. Coalition"
displays entries that represent the same opinion. If the slider
is set to the central position, all entries are displayed that have
something to do with the entry in the middle panel and whose
points in the Keyword Coordinate System tend to be in the
centre rather than at the extreme edges.

The programme evaluates the content that is present in an
entry and searches for entries that deal with the same topic.
Using the users' ratings and the entries in the Keyword
Coordinate System, the programme determines which entries
have favourable or unfavourable content. In the Keyword
Coordinate System, items that are in the same place are rated
as having the same opinion, and those that are opposite are
rated as having opposing opinions. Using the data of the
users, how they have rated which entries in the past and their
personal opinion in the coordinate system, it is determined
whether the user has the same or an opposing opinion.

Under the slider, the number of entries and persons with the
same or opposite opinion is displayed, depending on how the
slider is set. Below this display, all entries are listed one below
the other that are of the same or opposite opinion. The entries
that are most similar are shown at the top of the list if the
slider is set to "Coalition". If the slider is set to "Compromise",
the most dissimilar are displayed at the top. If the slider is in
the middle position, the most similar and the most dissimilar
are listed alternately, again depending on the strength of the
match.

The Connector allows users to check facts in entries. For
example, if an entry mentions the birth rate, the entries
on birth rates from the Statistical Office's intranet site are
displayed. If an author wants to include this data in his or
her entry, he or she can use the linker to take over the source
information.

14.5.7 Example view for Linker and Connector

Linker	Pinboard	Connector
Search source: [ ] Person, Group, Keywords, Date	Posts, comments and replies	----------------------I------ Compromise / Coalition Same entries: 25 Users with the same opinion: 8 Contrary entries: 46 Users with opposing opinions: 11
Search result:	Create your own post, comment or reply [Create].	Similar or opposite content:
Image / Name / Keyword Coordinate System / Date Content of the post, comment or reply <3 :D :0 :(:((+ - I_ ! P C A / Create quote ——— Source: Ministry, directory, profile, retrieval date, URL	Text Image Video Sound recording	Image / Name / Keyword Coordinate System / Date Similar content of a post, comment or reply <3 :D :0 :(:((+ - I_ ! P C A ... more similar content and less opposing content follows here because the slider is not quite on Coalition.

14.6 Image generator

The image generator helps to create title images for entries. These images are intended to serve as title pictures so that the subject of groups and reports can be quickly captured visually with pinboard progressions. To translate text into images, users can have a sentence or paragraph keyworded.

To do this, users type or copy the text to be illustrated into the text field at the top of the screen. The programme tags the text and displays images that match the keywords.

On the left under the text field, images matching each keyword are displayed. By swiping to the right or left, the pictures for a keyword can be turned forwards or backwards as in a wheel. In this way, you can select one or more pictures that you find suitable. There is a section in which all the pictures with the same background or as a cut-out are available so that they can be easily put together in a collage.

In the centre of the screen is the blank white image, i.e. the workspace. The image has the pixel size that is set as the requirement for cover images. The images from the left side can be transferred to this empty image, enlarged, reduced, cropped, rotated or deformed.

At the top right of the page are the tools for moving, scaling, rotating, cropping or deforming. At the bottom right, all the illustrations that are on the work surface are displayed as keywords one below the other. By default, they are listed word by word below each other in the order of the set. Depending on how far up you move one word above the other, this no longer makes grammatical sense, but it moves the image to the foreground on the work surface. In this way, a list is created from all the transferred illustrations as to which illustration is in the foreground or background. Similar to a tag cloud, the deciding factor is how many contributions fit a certain topic.

14.7 Indoor virtualiser

In order to depict reality, you can lend out Virtual Reality glasses and a 360° 3D helmet camera in the Intranet Café. The Virtual Reality glasses have a head-up display that shows you in real time how you move through the room and open doors and drawers. The glasses have a sliding cover so that you can immerse yourself completely in virtual reality. So you can immediately check the result and walk through the room with the shutter closed without bumping into anything. This allows you to move through your entire building or each room that you want to depict virtually. This can be either in the living room or at workplaces. However, no humans should be visible in the images and sufficient lighting should be provided. In order to be able to additionally virtualise objects, one has to look at the barcode or QR code on the product or packaging with the Virtual Reality glasses. Product information such as size, weight or function is automatically retrieved from the retailer's databases. Product information can also be entered by hand and keyboard if necessary.

Citizens and companies can use the indoor virtualiser to display their interiors in the virtual inland. Companies in the Planned Economy and Social Market Economy must use it. Owners of indoor spaces in buildings have the possibility to virtualise and store as many of their indoor spaces as they wish. They decide through their declaration of consent which parts of their indoor space should be visible to which persons in the intranet. Data that should not be displayed can be pixelated or blacked out by an additional programme in the indoor virtualiser.

14.7.1 Statistical evaluation

The Statistical Office is granted admission to the original data for anonymised statistical analysis. Other ministries must justify their retrieval by law. All state-collected data are strictly confidential and are only to be evaluated anonymously for economic simulation purposes. The rules on data protection prevent misuse. All data accesses are stored in the Access Directory.

This transparency of the citizen serves simulation purposes and the correctness of statistical data for state management. For state management of the national economy to be as error-free as possible, correct data is more important than a lot of data. With correct data, extrapolation can then be made. For indoor areas that are not virtualised, a statistical value is determined. The value is created by the data from the directories that are available about the building and the persons living or working in it. These are, for example, data from the tax account, electricity, data and water consumption. These data are supplemented with comparative values that come from virtualised indoor spaces.

15 Computer games

The highest maxim in the design of state computer games is that politics should be fun. Computer games are a form of play-giving that ensures that humans have fun and enjoyment by working together, but learn just as much in the process because they are productive. It is in play that new discoveries are most likely to emerge, this is how it is with children and this is how it is with adults. There is a desire in humans to play and to explore their environment through play and to be constantly curious. Nothing is more fun than playing together with other humans, as long as all participants want to play. The computer games of the Ministry of Digital Affairs make it possible to help shape the state, i.e. the organised coexistence of all citizens inland and across national borders.

The task of the Ministry of Digital Affairs is to provide suitable steering tools for the citizens. The goal should be to enable the population to control itself instead of electing humans to be controlled.

Every computer game is evaluated by the Ministry of Digital Affairs and flows into state statistics or management if the results are helpful. Every ministry is free to outsource policy decisions to games, such as the "tax game". As long as the whole people are affected, however, the environment of the majority may not be changed by a minority of players. However, if a quorum of 80% of all those affected is reached, binding decisions can be made. Laws, constitutional articles and elections of persons, however, must always be decided by real political procedures. The background to this is that even in the fully digital age, it remains important to see each other in person, especially when making policy decisions. Negotiations can be digitalised, but democratic electoral acts with consequences for the entire population that last for years must happen face to face with other citizens. Only then can citizens talk to each other and be motivated by the morally-minded electorate to vote only in ways that serve the common good. One should see the other humans who would be damaged by a wrong decision.

15.1 Avatar simulator

The avatar simulator allows users to create avatars that live a simulated life in the virtual inland. However, the virtual inland is a copy of the image from the People's Navigator. It is intended as a playground where invented avatars can let off steam at the user's discretion.

Each avatar can take a different path in life, sometimes placing more or less emphasis on sport, healthy eating, music, culture, pet ownership, family, politics, education, entrepreneurship or similar. What is decisive is what own data is fed into the new avatar and how closely this avatar coincides with the user's life path or is created for simulation purposes.

If the user creates several avatars, he can simulate several life paths at the same time and create save points whenever he wants. An automated function shows, for example, each educational path, where the avatar would have to go and when in order to complete a certain degree. The aim of this game is to be able to plan one's own life path in the best possible way because one has already simulated various possibilities.

15.1.1 Simulation view

The simulation view is the view of the satellite map of the inland from the People's Navigator. The data inputs can come from the different directories and can be entered daily in the control panel or retrieved automatically. The control panel is on the left side of the screen. Using a tree structure, one can select all one's own data individually or in groups and integrate them into the avatar's data set. The environment is the conventional real world of the country at the present time and all its possibilities of time design.

15.1.2 Virtual simulations

The statistical data in the virtual inland of the People's Navigator is not meant to be falsified by invented avatars. Rather, this simulation programme is a testing ground to virtually try out any career, invention or lifestyle. The simulations basically run in real time, but can be accelerated to double, tenfold or a hundredfold speed as long as the user presses the + key during the game. Requirements such as body stature, money or educational qualifications can be set by the user or users can import their own data. Each avatar is clearly assigned to its user and is thus not anonymous in the game. All other avatars of the user and avatars of other users of the simulation together form the simulation people.

15.1.3 Avatars

If users want to import their data, they can set the avatar to move in real time to where the user's People's Computer is currently located. Mobile add-on devices for the People's Computer are mobile phones or wristbands in which the location can be recorded. Users can import this data so that the avatar virtually moves to the appropriate locations. Using the data from the Health Directory, the avatar can obtain the identical physical constitution. All other data of the personal avatar in the People's Navigator, can also be imported.
If users prefer to create an avatar of their own design, they can do that too. The only requirement is that the avatar symbolises a human being. Everything else is up to the user.

15.1.4 Course of play

Users who want to change their body, for example, can test this virtually with the avatar simulator. One imports all the necessary data and can, for example, test sports with the avatar if they are overweight. The more precise the data entry, the more health problems can be displayed that could arise for a certain person during a certain type of sport. The data release is determined by each user. In this example, all data is retrieved from the Health Directory. In the case of overweight, it becomes clear how long a physical change would take the user. To do this, the avatar can, for example, go to the gym in the user's neighbourhood, provided the gym has digitised its service offerings and virtualised its indoor facilities. The avatar then uses the devices to train muscle groups and burn fat. If you also enter your avatar's food intake into the data set, you will get more accurate results. Food intake can be entered automatically if food purchases in markets or restaurants have been paid for digitally with the People's Bank bank card. The aim of this game play is to simulate physical training and nutrition virtually and to be able to achieve the physical change in reality, through better estimation of time and financial effort. The same process can be applied to any other operation that the avatar performs.

15.2 Tax game[77]

The tax game is a year-round supplement to the budget vote and is supported by the Ministry of Finance with the latest data. The programming is done by the Ministry of Digital Affairs on behalf of the Ministry of Finance.[78]

15.3 Algoracle[79]

The Algoracle is a simulation programme that is able to make predictions about the future. These can be future forecasts for private individuals, companies or the state, as was the case with the Oracle of Delphi. Behind these future predictions, however, are all the data of the intranet, algorithms and programme codes of the People's Innovation Company intranet and all the automatic machines active in the country. Reliable data from the internet and libraries complete the data set. Nevertheless, algorithms cannot be perfect, so a fundamental distrust is appropriate. On the other hand, the probability of encountering avoidable faults is increased.

---

77 §160.1 Financial Supervisory Authority: KV Art.106
78 Ministry of Finance - 9.6 Tax game
79 §207.6 Telecommunications, §71.2 Review of effectiveness

15.3.1 Purpose

The Algoracle serves the purpose of enabling the state to simulate policy deciders before they are implemented. In addition to the traditional statistics behind polls, the Algoracle makes it possible to correlate all digital data at the same time, thus enabling more precise statistical investigations. The simulation also includes all applicable laws. If a project violates laws or other norms, this is indicated and the simulation is terminated. The Statistical Office has access to all data and can thus calculate the most accurate forecasts of how the people can live in accordance with the common good. Since the state has once done this work, it can also make it available to its citizens and companies so that as few wrong decisions as possible are made.

15.3.2 Data processing

The Statistical Office obtains the necessary data to operate the Algoracle as reliably as possible. An algorithm processes the data and source codes of all machines active inland. It connects them in series, according to the real sequence of use, and keeps their data constantly up to date. All other necessary data, such as norms from the Law Directory, are entered into a programme so that the result can be seen in the virtual inland of the People's Navigator.

The simulator depicts the present time within the country's borders. The rules of the game can be changed with various adjusting screws, for example laws, tax increases or educational qualifications.

Results of simulations based on insufficient data sets are shown in a pale colour or it is explicitly pointed out in the presentation of results which data sets are insufficient or were filled by the algorithm due to insufficient data by extrapolating similar data. If the error quotient is above 1^{80} , several scenarios are shown in the result with their respective percentage probability.

80https://de.wikipedia.org/wiki/Fehlerquotient therein: Error density in computer science - see table

15.3.3 Data protection in the Algoracle

Especially the data from the intranet also contains sensitive personal data that must be protected. Therefore, only the state may access all data, provided that the law allows it to do so. However, it must inform the owners of this in the Access Directory and justify the access in the protocol. This also applies to all simulations of the Algoracle. In a simulation order, the data of many owners and People's Computers must be accessed. For this reason, a simulation order may be carried out by citizens and companies only in the intranet café, so that it is clear who wanted to simulate what. This is also to prevent People's Computers from accessing sensitive data en masse via radio signals. The intranet cafés ensure that the data is retrieved and only processed via the Algoracle's server to be output as a statistical result that does not allow any conclusions to be drawn about individuals' data.

15.3.3.1 Previous request for sensitive data

In the case of simulation orders that allow conclusions to be drawn about a person, citizens and companies must first obtain written consent from the affected owners of the data via the People's Computers. Thus, friendship or family relationships can be simulated if all persons affected consent to the project via their personal People's Computer. All economic and demographic key figures that are freely accessible are automatically included in the simulation.
A request to use data for the Algoracle can be sent to all profiles of all directories. The purpose of the simulation must be named and justified. Requested users can then disclose all or some of the requested data about themselves to support a particular research request. The data request commitments are sent from the owner's People's Computer to the requestor's People's Computer and to the Algoracle's server. Only then does the Algoracle request personal data.

15.3.4 Simulation order

Citizens and companies can prepare their simulation orders on the People's Computer, save all desired settings and, if necessary, send requests to affected persons. A simulation can be called up by the user for the following years or decades. Thus, one can simulate a friendship, marriage, training, professional career, the economic development of a new or existing company, the sales of a product or innovation, the success of a club in a certain place or even legislative initiatives. Profiles of persons, companies and products can be selected personally or automatically and inserted into the simulation order. Locations or perimeters must be specified or, if the best location for something is to be searched for, "best locations" is selected.

The saved settings can then be used on the Intranet Café computer to send the simulation order to the server. Once the simulation has been processed in the server and all the necessary data has been downloaded from People's Computers and processed, the simulation starts on the Intranet Café computer.

After the simulation, the file of the simulation can be downloaded to the user's own People's Computer so that the user can play the simulation repeatedly and create a simulation video. All downloaded People's Computer data is deleted from the server again after the simulation session in the Intranet Café.

15.3.5 Simulation of the Algoracle

The simulation is displayed on the computer in the intranet café in the People's Navigator view and played in 10-fold acceleration. In the simulation, predictions and development trajectories are shown for a person, a law, a company or a product. Different scenarios can be played through if they arise statistically. During the simulation, activities of the environment are displayed in fast forward from a bird's eye view. In the case of particularly decisive decisions, simulation is interrupted and the user is asked to make a decision.

The user can select a scenario from one of the displayed scenarios and thus continue the simulation. To select another scenario at a later time, the lower control panel can be unfolded to select the point in the tree structure and have the other path displayed as soon as the lower control panel is folded in again. The simulation ends as soon as it becomes too unlikely to be able to keep certain states unchanged for such a long time.

15.3.5.1 Scenarios

Often in simulations, decision questions can arise that are taken by the participants with a certain probability. If the probability here is less than 60%, a simulation must also be carried out for the remaining 40%. All decision questions that the creator of the simulation order can answer himself, because he is one of the participants in the simulation, are questioned. The questioning is done in real time on the computer of the intranet café because it is continuously calculated in the server. The calculated scenarios are displayed in a horizontal tree structure that grows like a timeline.

15.3.5.2 Reasons for a particular prediction

If the user wants to know the reasons for a particular prediction, he can pause the simulation at this point and open the lower control panel. Clicking on the path in the tree structure opens the data logbook. This lists all the data that the algorithm is currently accessing. Data that is not released for the user is automatically blacked out. If the user folds in the lower control panel again, he or she can change the view and move closer from a bird's eye view to select suitable sections of the map or specific persons, groups of persons or companies with a click or a rubber band frame.

If the data of the sources are released, an insight into the reasons for a prediction can be obtained. This makes it clear which data from an external user was decisive for a particular prediction. For example, if a project is doomed to fail because it is highly unlikely that a building permit would be granted, this reason can be shown because state agencies must always justify their reasons in the law. Private persons who have not released their sources can be asked by a personal message how they would act. If they have not even released their contact details, the reason cannot be determined.

15.3.6 Simulation video

In the virtual inland, all projects of the Algoracle can be filmed as a video. To do this, the user must specify which activities and persons affected are important and how long the video or film should last. In the virtual inland, all processes run in real time, in excerpts or in fast motion, depending on the specified duration. As the director, the user can stop the simulation to change perspectives, cut out parts of the real time or fast-forward through the time-lapse. Individual activities of affected citizens are shown in first-person perspective. Similar to the computer game Command and Conquer Generals[81] , the view is focused in or out from the bird's eye view into the first-person perspective. The user can thus direct the action, take different camera perspectives and show details that are significant to him in the simulation film in the appropriate perspective.

15.3.7 Comparison

Through various simulations and their comparison, competing projects can compete against each other. This makes it possible to see who benefits more or less from a programme or law. Citizens can have this represented for themselves or state television stations for a certain population group.

---

81 https://www.ea.com/de-de/games/command-and-conquer/command-and-conquer-generals

15.4 People-controlled politician[82]

With the computer game "People-Controlled Politician", citizens can exercise their superintendence over politicians directly via the intranet. Similar to the film "Nerve"[83] , the intranet is an alliance of directories from which data on political persons and events (players), but also opinions and ratings of citizens (watchers) are linked. In contrast to the game in the film or the app, it is not the order with the most money that is executed or rejected, but orders with the most approvals from those entitled to vote.

Politicians are induced here as players or participants to carry out political reforms or deeds that are beneath constitutional articles and laws.[84] Which acts the participants carry out and how, is decided by the citizens, spectators, instructors through their laws, proposals and their majority ratings. Every action of the politician is recorded by video. Possible courses of action are voted on in real time.

A politician can offer this procedure of direct management voluntarily by registering as a participant. However, this procedure can also be ordered by a committee. If special transparency is needed in a reform, this popular control can watch over the exact implementation and release the politician from responsibility. The politician can and may drop out at any time if he can no longer reconcile acts with his conscience. The computer game comes into play whenever popular empowerment is applied and can oblige politicians to participate.[85] Any offender is subject to constitutional allegiance.

82§70.3 Supervision: BV Art.169
83http://www.thenerveapp.com/how-to-play/ https://de.wikipedia.org/wiki/Nerve_%28Film%29
84Ministry of Justice - 4.6 Ladder of norms
85Ministry of State Organisation - 12.3 Popular empowerment

15.5 Policy Manager[86]

Citizens can administer (manage) political contents (policy) with their People's Computer through the game Policy Manger. The player takes on the role of a party member who participates in working groups or party wings, or the role of a member of a council of ministers or committee. The mission objective is always to solve a problem without causing damage and thereby improve the current state. The goal of a mission is either to create a quorum, a petition, an election programme, a citizens' initiative or a counter-template.[87] With this game, political contents are introduced into the democratic arena. The democratic arena, that is all the council buildings and public space in the virtual inland with all the intranet users online. The player fulfils his mission with any number of other players. The Policy Manager serves as a digital supplement to all political participation options for those entitled to vote. Parties and ministries can use the Policy Manager to digitise their work.

Users can view games in progress via a view mode without having to log in. Anyone who logs in can play immediately, provided they belong to the permitted group of persons. Should parties or ministries do their work in the Policy Manager, citizens have the possibility to force participation via a veto quorum through a committee, or they can start a mission in which they develop a Counter-template.

One starts the game by choosing an interesting problem and enough fellow players to solve it. After solution finding, the solution proposal is simulated, revised if necessary and then introduced into the election campaign to find majorities. Depending on how many votes are collected, the petition, citizens' initiative or counter-proposal can be submitted directly as a template or, if not enough supporters have been found in the election campaign, the solution proposal can be sent as a draft to the responsible minister or ministers.

86§94.5 Digital participation in committees
87Ministry of State Organisation - 9.5 Quorum, 9.10.11.6 Petition, 9.9.4.3 Election programme, 9.10.11.7 Citizens' initiative, 9.10.4 Counter-proposal

15.5.1 Playing field

The playing field is the People's Navigator view, but without all the avatars, unless they also play Policy Manager. In terms of its policy side, the game is a mixture of a committee, a council meeting, a working group of a party wing and a purely digital use of the show concept Solution Finder.[88] The game's presentation is a mixture of Second Life[89], facebook[90], Youtube[91], Google Earth[92], Command and Conquer[93], World of Warcraft[94] and Pro Evolution Soccer[95]. The user interface is the same three-dimensional satellite view of the inland as always in the People's Navigator.

The special feature is that during the game you only move around the map with the avatars of the other players. Only when a mission is in campaign mode do the players move their avatars in the People's Navigator with all the other avatars of the users of the intranet. The players' own avatar is then dressed in a campaign uniform that the players choose together. It is visible to other users that these avatars are in campaign mode.

15.5.1.1 Office

At the beginning of each game, each player is given an office. The office building is digitally inserted into the map and looks like a glazed cylindrical skyscraper. There are 4 offices on each floor and the lift is in the middle. The offices can be separated with partition walls or connected to form an office with 4 workstations. Depending on how many players are currently playing missions in a ministry, the more floors the skyscraper has.

---

88 Ministry of State Organisation - 9.6 Committee, 8.6 Councils, 8.5.6 Working Groups, Ministry of Media Affairs - 7.2.3.5 Solution Finder (Legislation Committee)
89 https://secondlife.com/
90 https://www.facebook.com/
91 https://www.youtube.com/
92 https://earth.google.com/web/
93 https://www.ea.com/de-de/games/command-and-conquer
94 https://worldofwarcraft.com
95 https://www.konami.com/wepes/2020/us/en-us/ps4/

The offices can be set up individually. In an editor, you have the option of selecting objects, inserting data from the indoor virtualiser and uploading pictures or videos to show your guest. Whether the office mutates into a living room depends on how much personal information the user wants to put online. Each office has a mailbox where news can be left when the player is not online.

15.5.2 Build player network

One first imports all the desired data of one's avatar from the People's Navigator. Then one can network with other players by exchanging business cards on which the virtual address of one's own office is linked. If the invitation is accepted, another avatar appears on the radar at the bottom left of the screen to make it easier to find each other. By arranging the networked avatars in specially created categories, selected groups can be displayed so that the radar remains clear.

15.5.3 Find problems

Every problem is the occasion for a mission, for which voluntary interested players come together. Depending on which ministry one is interested in, one selects it from the list of ministries. Via a link to the Legislative Directory, all new legislative projects in progress are displayed. These real missions can be taken over as missions in the game. A link to the Law Directory and Quorum Directory can be used to display laws and politicians whose repeal quorum or deselection quorum will soon be fulfilled. This can become a mission for an initiative or an election programme. Players can also develop new missions themselves by collecting problems. A list of problems then appears, which players compile and rate problems on the list as important or unimportant. Players can also add their own new problems here and wait until enough other players find them important. If you read through the list of important problems, you will also see how many players have indicated that they want to play this mission. You can also do this. While looking through the list, you can rate the problems you read as important and unimportant and put a tick if you want to play this mission. Next to the box with the tick is a display. Here you can see how many players are needed for the mission and how many players have already indicated that they want to play this mission.

15.5.3.1 Ongoing missions

Under the problem list is an overview of ongoing missions. You can play along there. If a desired mission, for which one had agreed to play along, is ready to start, one is asked whether one wants to play along or join in later. These new reports are displayed in the right-hand control panel. The control panel informs the player of all upcoming missions in which he has expressed interest.

With the Policy Manager, players can also participate in all political events in the People's Navigator. For this purpose, the player can teleport his People's Navigator avatar to the location of the event. For example, a committee takes place in a city far away from the citizen. The citizen can then either watch the broadcast on Government Television[96] and participate via his People's Computer or he can participate digitally via the People's Navigator with his avatar.

15.5.3.2 Areas of accountability

Depending on the problem at hand, responsibility may lie with a municipality or only a certain group of persons may be affected, for example consumers, villages or companies. In these cases, the person who publicises the problem can define a group of persons who are allowed to participate.

For example, for a political reform that affects only one village, only the villagers are admitted as players. In this case, the game is held in the virtual plenary hall of the responsible town hall. Anyone who works in a company and identifies a policy problem there can enter it in the problem list of the Ministry

------

96Ministry of Media - 7 Government Television

of Economy in which the company is registered. If the Ministry of Planned Economy were responsible, the mission would be set in the capital city of that ministry. The group of persons playing could then be limited to all members of the Planned Economy, to residents of a Social Village or to the employees of the affected company. Indoor spaces that have been virtualised can also be used as a playing field.

15.5.4 Find solutions

All meetings are open to the public. However, only Policy Manager players who have registered in this mission are entitled to vote. New registrations are possible at any time so that users can join the current mission and access the results so far. For solution finding, the players meet in the arena of the responsible ministry, elect a leader, speak for or against and present drafts and amendments. At the end, solutions found are simulated and revised if the simulation did not go in the players' favour.

15.5.4.1 Arena

The places where players come together to find a majority solution are called arenas. The arenas are the council buildings where parties or councils usually meet and have been digitally recreated with the indoor virtualiser. An arena is located in the capital city of the ministry responsible for the problem or in the town hall of a municipality. Each player has a seat in the arena. There, speeches are held to find and justify solutions. The players work on the solution text with the help of the Negotiator from the Modulator.

15.5.4.2 Leader

The leader of an arena during the mission, is elected by the fellow players and is in office until the quorum of 50% of all mission participants calls for a new election. Candidates are all voluntary members of the mission. The leader adds players to the list of speakers and allocates speaking time. Motions for new agenda items are submitted to him.

15.5.4.3 Media library

All contributions and speeches in the arenas are recorded and stored in the game's media library so that players can view missed speeches and contributions at any time. In each arena, the Solution Finders' participation options are permanently valid[97] . Some opportunities are only available in the livestream, but no longer in the media library. As long as a mission is running, all speeches can be rated and commented on by players and spectators. Afterwards, all mission data can only be viewed. Each player can see in the statistics which speech was viewed by which target group and how often. The target groups result from the anonymised data of the spectators and are sorted by age, gender, income and educational qualification.

15.5.4.4 Speech

Players give speeches in the arenas. Players can upload these speeches to the media library at any time, but they are only given in the arena when it is their turn. Each proposed solution is discussed, rated, reformulated and rated again in the arena by the community of players. This continues until a majority solution has been worked out. The point of each speech is to clarify the text for the proposed solution. In a speech for, arguments for a formulation can be given, in a speech against, the opposite.

A player may not be able to obtain certain information easily. In that case, requests can be sent to the Federal Moderator's Office or the responsible state research institute.[98] Some work processes may not be known to a player. They are presented in the Knowledge Directory in articles from Party Television[99] .

---

97 Ministry of Media Affairs - 7.2.3.5 Solution Finder (Legislation Committee)
98 Ministry of State Organisation - 4.4 Federal Moderator's Office, Ministry of Education - 11.7.2 State Research Institutes
99 Ministry of Media - 10 Party Television

With the help of this information, players can compare their moves with realpolitik.

Speeches in the arenas must always include images, sounds or videos and not just text. Each speaker has a large screen for presentations and animations. For example, videos can describe a process or posters can present a solution to a problem. During the virtual speech, the user's avatar speaks in the arena. Players deliver the speech in front of their People's Computer and have themselves filmed against a fixed background. Their face is automatically cut out and inserted into the avatar's face. The camera recognises hand movements and the programme simulates them on the avatar. All videos and audio contributions can be commented on and rated by players and viewers down to the second by right-clicking on the timeline, as is possible, for example, with soundcloud[100] . In this way, a player can collect advocates for his idea. For speeches, ratings can be given by all fellow players. Those who receive more positive ratings for their speeches are more likely to determine the content of the solution path.

15.5.5 Simulation of the solution

Once a solution is ready, its consequences are simulated by the Algoracle. The problem and the proposed solution are entered into the Algoracle. As soon as chaos breaks out in the virtual inland because everyone behaves according to the new rule, the test is considered failed. Players can look up in this simulation when, why and where the first unrest occurred. After newly making adjustments, the test can be repeated.

If the test is positive, the election campaign phase begins, in which sufficient supporters must be found among the users of the intranet.

---

100 https://soundcloud.com/avidmuzikfan2/eric-prydz-live-tomorrowland-2018

15.5.6 Election campaign mode

In election campaign mode, players no longer find majorities on the playing field, but on the virtual map in the People's Navigator. Ready-made proposals for solutions are filmed as simulation videos and used to collect votes from citizens. No matter where the players conduct their opinion or election campaign, they present their proposed solutions as appealingly and multimedia-based as possible.

The length of the campaign phase is newly determined by all players for each mission in a voting, similar to doodle[101] . In the voting, periods or times for appointments are found together in a group.

15.5.6.1 Vote catching

Vote-catching takes place exclusively on the intranet. Players contact users of the intranet, So-called passers-by, via their avatars in the People's Navigator, in directories, via pinboards or personal news. There they present the proposed solution and can collect supporters via a virtual signature list. Players publish posts on pinboards that include a voting for an opinion on the proposed solution. Those who vote for it automatically place their digital signature. During the campaign phase, sufficient supporters must be found. The number of supporters needed depends on the number of persons affected. Digital signature lists are also accepted alongside handwritten ones in order to provide the necessary number of those entitled to vote, for example, to put an initiative, petition or quorum to the vote.

15.5.6.2 New proposals

During an election campaign phase, new proposals for solutions are possible through passers-by. Passers-by are users who do not want to play Policy Manager but are contacted by players via the People's Navigator. All new incoming solution proposals are collected and evaluated by the players, grouped and simulated as new input by the algroacle. If the test is

---

101https://doodle.com/de/

positive, they are released for the election campaign. In this case, the campaign phase can be extended. However, this may only happen 3 times, otherwise the mission is considered a failure and must be restarted.

15.5.6.3 Election campaign events

Election canvassing can be done in virtual public places through digital events. The players prepare and conduct these events together. In order to quickly travel with their avatars between public places on the map, players can teleport their avatars. Should a public place in the virtual world become overcrowded because there are too many avatars there, new levels are drawn in the sky on which the avatars float. If several virtual events are taking place in a public place at the same time, the users can decide which event they want to show and which they want to hide. This also automatically hides all avatars of participants of hidden events.

Players can register events by marking a radius on the map and indicating from when to when they are holding an event there. The computer game automatically sends a request to the People's Navigator to release the area for the event. Events already registered within this radius are displayed in a list during the registration process. The organisers can then change either the location or the date of their event.

15.5.7 Mission Goal

A mission ends when it has been abandoned or successfully completed. Any solution that has been democratically formulated by the players, successfully simulated by the Algoracle and achieved the necessary approval of 30% of the affected citizens in the campaign phase is now sent to the responsible politician. The mission is now successfully completed. If the approval ratings are higher, quorums can also be triggered with it or proposals can be introduced. As is usual with voting, the votes are held in an election week at the voting computer in the town hall.

If the approval ratings are lower, it is up to the responsible politician whether the proposed solution is implemented, rejected or voted on with the affected citizens. If the proposed solution is implemented, it can be seen from the text which idea came from which person. In this way, ministries, political parties and authorities can contact the author of an idea directly, regardless of whether he or she is a player in "Policy Manager" or has contributed as a passer-by. This contact with the original author becomes important if there are queries in the legislative process or state implementation. If the idea comes in whole or in part from a comment by a user or other player, the passage is automatically marked and cited as a source in the document that is sent to the minister. Inventors of an idea, whether players or users in the commentary, must be invited to the panel when it comes to the committee. This is to avoid misunderstandings and misinterpretations.

15.5.8 Remuneration

When the proposal finds its policy implementation in the real world, the responsible politicians give a certain amount of points to the authors of the proposed solution. Each accepted proposal is remunerated at a flat rate and has two bonus levels. The first level is the number of persons affected. The second level is the success rate during the future existence. Thus, a point amount is permanently paid out via the second stage. Failure in voting and subsequent implementation costs points. If an applied solution proposal is put out of action, the inflow of points ceases. The office of the leader brings a standard monthly amount of winning points, which depends on the number of participants in the mission. One point is awarded for each voting and 1000 points are awarded for each statement of one's own that went into the formulation of a law.
Realpolitik is thus the virtual source of winning points and measures the success of solution proposals and idea generators. These winning points are used by players to improve their rank. Those who have a high rank will be a popular contributor in discussions and election campaigns and are known to the

parties and ministries as productive Solution Finders. Winning points are forfeited by the death of a fellow player or by the deletion of the avatar by the user.

15.5.9 Game variations

Further variations become necessary when political contents take place abroad. As a component of international relations, at least the international institutions, such as the United Nations[102] and the Continental Union, are represented virtually.
In this variant the United Nations plenary assembly are created in specially made three-dimensional maps of New York. The interiors of the government buildings necessary for the game are recreated virtually.

15.6 Psychotherapy game

A non-binding offer for self-therapy is the psychotherapy game, in which one first tests oneself in order to be able to create the appropriate game course on the basis of the test results. In the psychotherapy game, strokes of fate are played out in missions. The first mission is to live through one's own fate. Players are asked about their CV in a questionnaire and thus determine the content of the first mission. After the first mission, the CV is compared with all other similar CVs of psychologically treated people and a game character is created that is similar to all these humans. In the following missions, the character lives through the fates of other patients and their successful treatment in a virtual world.
Scientists from the psychology departments of all state colleges are used to create the algorithm and keep it up-to-date. This is done by the developers retrieving all the data of all those working in psychology via the Health Directory and evaluating it by an algorithm. In the data, CVs are linked to psychological illness symptoms and therapy methods and which method led to healing for which CV or symptom. It

---

102https://www.un.org/en/

looks at which descriptions resulted in which treatment and how many sessions with which physicians and psychologists were necessary and whether a cure was achieved or not.

15.6.1 Treatment missions

In the first mission, the player processes his or her own life history and transfers it into an avatar, which becomes the player's character. Depending on which experiences in childhood and growing up from 0 to 30 years of age have shaped one's life positively or negatively, the temperament and opinion of the game character is adjusted by the programme. During the test, the players also describe the best and worst events of their lives as well as their mental illness symptoms. One lives through one's own biography with the player character and can select by hook how one felt and when. For all the situations described by the players, suitable virtual situations are created by an algorithm based on all the statements in the introductory tests of all the players.

The players' text input about their best and worst life events is keyworded and contextualised by the algorithm. With the help of the avatar simulator, one's own life course is simulated, psychologically analysed, explained and provided with advice. It is shown how beautiful or bad strokes of fate can be processed and dealt with. As soon as one has played through one's CV, the first mission is finished.

The character is now ready to face new situations in further missions. The missions consist of strokes of fate that other humans have experienced and have developed similar mental disorders as a result and have been successfully treated. In the game, own situations will appear that the players themselves have experienced, others not. These other situations are situations of other players that other players have experienced and show similar symptoms. In response to the question of what should happen after the blow of fate, the programme offers successful treatment methods of psychological practice. Thus, one can no longer do what one did oneself after the blow of fate, but the game characters always experience the life courses that successfully treated humans have experienced after a blow of fate, including psychological treatments.

15.7 Second Earth

The purpose of this game is to find a planet that is so similar to Earth that humanity and Earth's nature can survive there once Earth no longer exists. This game can be played on the internet and intranet. All usable data from observation stations on Earth and in outer space will be packaged into a simulator through appropriate programming, which will make the search appealingly visual for players. The programme is to be designed in such a way that existing data are evaluated with the help of the computing power in the player's computer. So far, the lack of sufficient computing power and persons to analyse the data has been the bottleneck that has made progress in the search for a second Earth slow. The game is there to change that. Players' computers receive data sets, which are processed by their computers and sent back to the research lab from which they received the data sets. This increases the computing power. By visualising the data, players can search the universe that has already been mapped. All parts already searched cannot be searched more than 3 times by different players. Whoever finds an Earth-like planet has the right to name it after himself. Finders report their find immediately via the lower control panel. The programme automatically sends the necessary data to the research laboratories, which check the find. Every confirmed find is reported in the news on state television. If enough players participate, they can raise money through crowdfunding to set up new observation stations in space or expand existing ones.

15.8 Educational game[103]

The educational game is a joint project of the ministries of digital, education and media. The Ministry of Education ensures the scientifically tested quality of the content. The Ministry of Digital Affairs ensures the programming of the

---

103 §182.2 Further education: BV Art. 64a

practical application and provision on the People's Computer, in the intranet café or in prisons.

This game uses the Knowledge Directory to help the player answer questions or complete missions. Questions are short pieces of information and work steps in the educational game, such as how to bake a certain cake. Missions include degrees and certificates that can be obtained at state educational institutions by passing a final exam.

The learning game uses the results of the assessment test[104] to determine the player's initial level of knowledge. An algorithm continuously searches the player's own profiles in all directories during the game. After the questions are asked or before the missions, short tests are carried out to adapt the answers or tasks to the level of knowledge. This is intended to teach laypersons things from the beginning and to spare those with advanced training the introductions. Players can also deactivate the test of their own level of knowledge or adapt it to other levels of education or age groups.

15.8.1 Aim of the Educational Game

The aim of the game is to be able to answer simple and complicated questions of life through education. The more educational experience a player gains through tests and final examinations, the more points he achieves in his education account. For the education rank, the total number of points always applies. For specialisation, the score per education area applies.

The educational subject areas are based on the subject areas and the social and economic sectors. Depending on the keywording, missions fit several subject areas or sectors.

15.8.2 Level

Every question that is viewed, every mission that is completed and every educational qualification that is virtually examined and every test that is successfully passed earns points and

---

104 Ministry of Education - 12.7.4 Assessment Test

ensures promotion to a higher level. A player's overall level indicates the user's level of education and is made up of knowledge sorted by different subject areas and industries.

15.8.3 Avatar in the educational game

The player's avatar has the same school-leaving qualifications, work experience, certificates, private further education and club experience as the player himself, and all other players can see this. The game receives the data from the Education Directory, Labour Directory, Club Directory and Persons Directory and maps it into a profile for each avatar.

The player's own avatar from the People's Navigator serves as the game character. As a player, you move your avatar around the virtual inland and steer to educational institutions or companies that give you admission to the necessary knowledge or materials to complete a mission. The learning game has the view of the People's Navigator, but takes place on its own playing field. All other avatars from the People's Navigator are visible but pale in colour. Avatars who are engaged in an activity that has a profile in the Knowledge Directory appear dotted. If you speak to them as a player, you can find out directly how their activity works and learn it.

The persons you have to visit in the course of your mission are shown in the radar at the bottom of the left control panel. The necessary workshops are displayed in your vicinity. You can virtually enter any company that has given you permission to do so and observe the avatars as they work. Once you have learned the work steps, you can click to send the avatars aside and operate the machines yourself. Companies can give the go-ahead when their indoor spaces are fully virtualised. Planned Enterprises are required to give clearance. For each machine, there are training videos or operating instructions from their manufacturers. This content is imported from the Knowledge Directory and allows instructions to be displayed through the Virtual Reality glasses. The manufacturing activities are carried out by the player in the first-person perspective, which also makes it possible to focus very closely. The necessary instructions on how to operate something are given via the Virtual Reality glasses.

15.8.4 Editor

If a learning content has not been virtualised using real models, players of the learning game can build their own virtual models in which any work process can be simulated. Rooms can be built in an editor and a virtual machine park is available that fits the respective automation. If certain machines are required, they can be selected from the catalogue of the Procurement Office[105] or from the Labour Directory. The same applies to raw materials. Now the player has a virtual room, tools and raw materials for the virtualisation of a learning content in order to be able to create a new mission.

15.8.5 Practical exercises and exams

For many missions, equipment is needed to immerse in a virtual reality to complete practical parts of a training virtually. The equipment is produced by the People's Innovation Company Intranet and includes tools such as Virtual Reality glasses, sensor clothing and remote controls, for movement. The equipment can be bought or lent out from the intranet café.

In missions that represent state qualifications for education and training, practical examinations must be taken in the intranet café. For this purpose, the examinee wears the sensor clothing and Virtual Reality glasses and performs actions with virtual elements on a delimited area. They are filmed by 4 cameras. This image material is automatically evaluated. The programme uses a recording of certified professionals who have virtualised this task as a sample. During the virtualisation, the professionals wear the sensor clothing and the Virtual Reality glasses. The 4 cameras record the movements of the professionals and the result of their activity. If the movements are similar to those of the professional and the result looks the same, the test is passed.

---

105 Ministry of Labour - 6 Procurement Office

Having passed the theoretical and practical tests, one can immediately register for any final examination of state educational institutions. If you pass the final exam, you receive the educational qualification without ever having attended real classes.

15.8.6 Questions

Players enter questions using the search function in the left-hand control panel. To narrow down the search result, you can enter what you intend to do and which education subjects might be responsible for it in the search field of the advanced search.

Questions are answered by the programme's access to the entire Knowledge Directory. Each profile can be accessed instantly. For example, there is no need to search carpentry training until the video on how to attach a table leg comes up. Because each learning content has been extensively keyworded, the algorithm can quickly find the right profiles in the wealth of all state training programmes.

Questions can be simple or complicated. Simple questions would be, for example: How do I screw on a table leg? Why do teeth fall out? Complex questions from the same areas would be: What do I need to know to be a carpenter? What does a dentist know about teeth? More complex questions can go over several missions and include several educational qualifications.

Once a question has been answered, a short test is offered afterwards in which questions are asked about the answer. This test checks whether the answer was correctly understood. If the test result is correct, the player receives points for his account for level advancement.

15.8.7 Missions

The player decides on the task he or she likes best or an undertaking he or she has in mind. Missions are completed by demonstrating activities from industries and knowledge from subject areas. Test tasks to the player check whether sufficient knowledge is available to start a mission with the specified learning content.

15.8.7.1 Learning groups

All players who play the same or a similar mission with the same learning content are linked together in a learning group. There they can exchange information and compare learning content and projects. In the virtual view, the learning groups consist of the avatars of the players who meet in their nearest educational institution in the virtual classroom or laboratory.

15.8.7.2 Create missions

Player-created missions are designed to implement larger projects, such as starting a company or building a house. Players can create their own missions. They enter a search in the left-hand control panel and look for suitable profiles from the Knowledge Directory. All missions are saved. These missions are also displayed in the search if other players have previously had similar missions. Missions can be rated and improved by players. Improvements can be made by recording new training videos or by compiling more suitable profiles from the Knowledge Directory. Popular missions lead more often to successful undertakings. In this way, players of the educational game expand the curricula for different subjects and combine subjects into undertakings. The Institute of Education audits the missions and can propose successful missions for the state curriculum. Examinations Offices can use it to compile project exams more easily.[106]
For example, a mission could be: Build your own house. At the beginning of the mission, you then design your house as a virtual walk-in three-dimensional model. Depending on the type of construction and equipment, you only have to learn certain work steps and not all the different ways of building

---

106Ministry of Education - 4.4.2 Curriculum Development, 4.6 Examinations Office, 4.6.1.1 Project Examination

a wall, for example. If it is to be a mud house, you only learn how to build with mud and not with wood or concrete.

15.8.7.3 Mission history

Each mission includes the following steps. First, you learn theoretically what you have to do to achieve the mission objective. Secondly, you have to practically perform the appropriate action in the virtual inland with your avatar in order to achieve the mission objective. Thirdly, you explain to a fellow player with a lower level how to master the exam that you yourself last passed. If the examinee passes the exam, his mentor also receives points.

In the theoretical phase, players should consume learning content from the Knowledge Directory, practice, test and form learning groups in which they help each other or share the work.

In the practical phase, the player goes with his avatar or real to institutions that deal with his field of learning and imitates their work. Or one is supposed to join project groups with other players of this game and find mentors. Mentors are fellow players who are a few levels ahead of the player. Depending on how successful tests are, there are different tasks. The tasks are adapted to the player's learning type[107] and enable social contacts, if necessary also via video conference. Some missions require a real practical test, which is conducted in the intranet café.

15.8.7.4 Trainings

Pre-prepared missions are the learning content and performance records of all state educational institutions and are designed to be able to take virtual degrees. Virtual degrees can be taken as a fun element after each set of tasks, which also serve as exam preparation for real degrees.

Among the saved missions, one has the possibility to choose an educational course including a degree. The Ministry of

---

107 Ministry of Education - 5.11.2 Learning Type Test

Education ensures that digitised education is guaranteed and that all courses for degrees at state educational institutions can be played as missions.

At the beginning, the player indicates his preferences for subject areas. Based on these requirements and the data from the Persons Directory and the Education Directory, the player's prior knowledge and interests are calculated. Learning content is recommended one after the other, depending on the level of education entered in the Education Directory. This avoids overtaxing or undertaxing the player. As a result, the algorithm offers several educational paths for the player. Now the player himself can create his educational path and his curriculum from virtual courses and decide when he wants to learn what and how. At the end of each educational path is a goal that the player chooses himself. This goal can be a final examination, an internship, a job, a product, a service or an honourary service.

15.8.7.4.1 Theory

In the theoretical phases, there are learning videos, podcasts and texts. Each medium on its own is capable of conveying the learning material that will be tested later. Each unit is concluded with a short multiple choice test immediately after the consumption of the medium. This test is used to determine whether one was attentive enough during media consumption. These short tests are necessary to gain further knowledge that builds on the previous knowledge. If the new knowledge could not be applied yet, the algorithm automatically repeats the unit and offers alternative tasks and learning methods for the same content. These tests are exported to the Knowledge Directory as a standard application so that users can test their knowledge level to get better search results in the Knowledge Directory.

At the end of an entire lesson, there is again a multiple-choice test, but it is longer and contains more complex questions. The tests are structured as games in which the questions are packaged in stories that the game characters experience, continuously asking the player test questions that match the scenario.

15.8.7.4.2 Practice

In the practical phases, things are bought, organised or done in order to produce something, or to work somewhere in the real world. Depending on the educational pathway, this is, for example, asking a particular teacher at a school, doing a work placement or selling a product via the intranet. Practical phases are simulated with Virtual Reality glasses and sensor clothing. This turns the learning game into the game that is also used in prisons, where the prisoners only have their single cell.[108] The function of being able to exchange with other players and avatars is not available to prisoners in order to prevent the risk of escape.

16 Switching to the new system

The changeover to the new system takes place step by step. The first step is to use the internet and all devices that can access the internet. The available free open source programmes are used and intranet cafés are instituted. In the second step, operating systems and programmes for the intranet are written, lines are laid and production facilities for the People's Innovation Company Intranet and People's Computer are built on stock. The third step is to hand out the People's Computers to schools first, before they can be bought at production price from the intranet café 6 months later.

16.1 Information Technology departments

All Information Technology departments of all ministries are transferred to the Ministry of Digital Affairs. The former workers of the Information Technology departments will henceforth work in the digital service. The digital service ensures the conversion to digital administration in the ministries. For this purpose, in the first step, all non-digital data will be photographed or scanned and included in the

---

108 Ministry of Justice - 7.5.11 Further education

state archives. The digital state archives are also transferred to the state archives of the digital administration. In the second step, the new computer programmes for digital administration are programmed and introduced. In the third step, the directories are set up to the extent that the digitally administered ministries can network and collaborate digitally.

16.2 Operating systems and programmes

All tax-funded computers inland are operated with the Linux operating system and only open source programmes from the open source community[109] , such as Open Office, Mozilla Firefox and Thunderbird, may be used. Only if no open source programme is available may programmes be purchased. All programmes that have already been purchased may continue to be used, provided that the licences do not have to be renewed in a subscription. All programmes that still have to be subscribed to because there are no open source programmes available will be put out to tender for programming. Prize money will be offered to anyone who is the first to provide a replacement programme. The replacement programme must be open source and free for all. The prize money comes from a provision that state users of licensed software subscribed to have to make. The provision accrues each time the recurring amount of the subscription becomes due. The amount of the provision is as much as the cost of the subscription, which doubles the cost and causes the provision to steadily increase. The current amount of the prize money is announced monthly in News Television .[110]

16.3 Programming in an alliance

State schools and colleges are programming the new software. First, all learners are familiarised with the open-source programmes and operating systems in the subjects of computer science. Afterwards, Internet pages are programmed for the

---

109https://opensource.org/
110Ministry of Media - 8 News Television

Ministry of Digital Affairs, through which all the necessary programmes for citizen participation are available as an Internet application. Based on open source operating systems and programmes, the tools for the show concept Solution Finder[111] are programmed, directories, the People's Navigator in 2D without avatars and the Policy Manager. Pirate parties[112] from all over the world already have programmes for digital political processes that are freely available and only need to be adapted slightly to the new system.

The subject of computer science in the comprehensive school and the computer science programmes in the colleges conduct performance records at least 4 times a year in which subsections are programmed. The level of difficulty of the sub-sections of all the above-mentioned programmes is tailored to the skills by learning year. Accordingly, all performance records are different and allow for rapid programming in the national alliance. The alliance is led by the most capable computer science chairs at state universities and colleges. SAP consultants can assist them, provided that SAP agrees to the terms and conditions and uses only open source software and programs if necessary.

Once all the necessary applications are available, a new operating system, all the programmes and computer games of the Ministry of Digital Affairs are programmed.

16.4 Terminal devices

As long as the People's Computer is not available and no intranet lines are laid, the programmes already programmed will work via the Internet, computers and mobile phones. All functions are available via the Ministry of Digital Affairs' website after one has registered. To register, one must photograph one's identity card and agree to data retrieval from the state civil registers.

---

111 Ministry of Media Affairs - 7.2.3.5.5 Participation for viewers
112 https://www.piratenpartei.de/partei/piratenparteien-international/

16.5 Directories

The first directories are the Persons Directory, Labour Directory and Quorum Directory. The Persons Directory bundles all data from all civil registers. The Labour Directory takes over all data from the Employment Offices. The Quorum Directory is initially only representative if the connection security cannot yet be guaranteed. Ministries gradually introduce directories as they are converted to the new system. As soon as a ministry is converted, the necessary directories are also created.

16.6 Intranet café

Until a town hall has an intranet café in place, an office in the town hall will be used. There, citizens and companies are given advice on which devices they can use the new functions with and participate in collective orders for the suitable devices. They also receive help with the installation of open-source operating systems and programmes.
Intranet cafés will be instituted in all town halls. Until the lines for the intranet are laid, a secured and, if possible, shielded area on the internet will be used as a temporary intranet. Initially, only the computers in the intranet café can access the temporary intranet.

16.7 Statistical Offices

All state statistical offices are transformed into the Statistical Office. It collects all data collected in ministries and evaluates them according to new and old national economic indicators.

16.8 Conversion of the old ministries

For the conversion of the old ministries, all departments and units of the old ministries that are changing to this ministry are identified. The organigrams are used to determine whether an entire department and all its units are changing or only individual units. All unsuitable departments and units are dropped. The existing staff adapts its tasks to the new requirements.

Contact form

Dear reader
If you would like to make what you have read come true, in whole or in part, together with other like-minded people, I offer you several possibilities with this contact form. Fill it out, tear out the page and send it by post to:
Andreas Seidl, P.O. Box 1206, 63488 Seligenstadt / Germany

Or send the details to:
Phone: 0049 1522 818 2243 (whatsapp, telegram, signal)
Email: andreas.seidl2022@web.de

Please mark with a cross:
O   I want to found a dynamic People's Party.
O   I want to donate money for implementation.
O   I want contacts with like-minded people in my area.

Forename: ___________________________________

Surname: ___________________________________

Please fill in only the contact option through which a reply should be made.

Street, house no.:   _______________________________

Postcode, city, country: _______________________________

Phone: _______________________________

Email address: _______________________________